D1482573

STRATEGIC PLANNING

A HUMAN RESOURCE TOOL
FOR HIGHER EDUCATION

Edited by Kathleen M. Alvino, M.B.A.

COLLEGE AND UNIVERSITY PERSONNEL ASSOCIATION
WASHINGTON, DC

About CUPA

Established 50 years ago, the College and University Personnel Association (CUPA) is an international network of more than 6,100 human resource administrators serving almost 1,700 colleges and universities.

The Association promotes the effective management and development of human resources in higher education. CUPA provides a forum for the exchange of ideas through annual conventions, workshops, and seminars; annual research and analysis on administrative and faculty salaries, benefits, and other surveys and special study reports; and periodicals, monographs, books, and videotapes on topics of interest to human resource practitioners.

Through its national office in Washington, DC, the Association keeps its members abreast of the most recent judicial decisions affecting human resource management and communicates that information to members through columns such as "Legal Watch" in the semimonthly newsletter, *CUPA News.* Additionally, CUPA provides members legislative information through "Legislative Update" and "Legislative Tracker" columns in *CUPA News.* To keep members up to date on the latest benefits information, the Benefits Information Program, administered by the CUPA Foundation, supplies "Benefits Watch" columns in *CUPA News* along with *Special Reports* and *Benefits Alerts*, which are mailed as events happen.

The Board of Directors, composed of elected regional and national officers from CUPA member institutions, provides governance and leadership to the Association. CUPA offers seven types of membership—Institutional, Individual, Retiree, Student, Associate, International Associate, and Corporate.

To learn more about membership in CUPA or any of its publications, please call 202-429-0311.

Cover design by Arna - Faces, Rhode Island School of Design

Table of Contents

Acknowledgments   *page iv*

Preface   *page v*

About the Authors   *page vi*

1   *What Is Strategic Planning?*   *page 1*
G. Gregory Lozier

2   *What Is the Problem You Are Trying to Solve?*   *page 21*
John A. Dunn, Jr.

3   *Begin at the Beginning*   *page 35*
Felice D. Billups

4   *What about Budgeting?*   *page 45*
James H. Manifold

5   *Rightsizing*   *page 57*
Kathleen M. Alvino

6   *Faculty and Staff Benefits: Meeting the Challenge of Difficult Financial Times*   *page 71*
Robert M. Wilson

7   *Total Quality Management Principles and Strategic Planning*   *page 83*
Deborah J. Teeter & G. Gregory Lozier

8   *Keeping the Plan Alive*   *page 105*
K. Scott Hughes

Acknowledgments

I would like to express my sincere appreciation to the authors of this book. Despite workloads, travel schedules, and unforeseen illnesses, each persevered to complete the work.

Thanks to each of them for his or her diligence, enthusiasm, patience, and sense of humor.

Preface

"The end is nothing; the journey is everything; and planning is the journey."—A Wise Old Planner

Strategic planning is a living, breathing process. As George Keller noted in the 1983 book, *Academic Strategy: The Management Revolution in American Higher Education*, strategic planning was the chosen method for colleges and universities to meet the changing economic and demographic conditions of the 1980s. Strategic planning is still being practiced and is still seen as the best method for providing the parameters, guidelines, and benchmarks to support the vision of an institution.

Strategic planning in higher education has been theorized, analyzed, and argued in terms of its success or failure. This book is composed of chapters authored by knowledgeable researchers and practitioners who view strategic planning as an essential element in the life of a successful college or university.

The chapters provide guidance to human resource professionals on how to become a viable part of an institution's strategic planning process and how to use strategic planning to promote the human resource function as a cornerstone in a successful planning process.

This book begins by defining strategic planning and explains how to identify the core problems the college or university wants to address and solve through the planning process. The book proceeds with advice on how to: begin the process, define the role of budgeting, plan for "rightsizing" the work force, and plan for management of faculty and staff benefits during difficult financial times. The book concludes with two chapters, one on the relationship of strategic planning and the total quality management process, and the final on how to keep the strategic planning process alive.

We hope the purpose of this book—to provide human resource practitioners with a clear, practical, structural approach to strategic planning—builds a foundation for the human resource function to be a viable partner in an institution's planning process.

About the Authors

Kathleen M. Alvino, M.B.A., is Director of Human Resources at the Rhode Island School of Design (RISD). At RISD since 1989, she has directed the development, implementation, and integrity of programs and policies including compensation, benefits, labor relations, recruitment, affirmative action, workers' compensation and loss prevention, training, organizational development, and communications. She has directed the human resource function and conducted labor contract negotiations in England, Scotland, and Canada. Alvino is a consultant in the areas of compensation, benefit management, and employee/labor relations for various colleges and companies. Her affiliations with professional organizations include the College and University Personnel Association, the Personnel Management Council of Greater Providence, the American Compensation Association, and the New England Society for Personnel Management. Alvino received her M.B.A. from Northeastern University in human resources management, specializing in organizational design and development. She also received her B.S. in personnel and industrial relations from Northeastern.

Felice D. Billups, Ed.D., has been Director of Planning and Research at the Rhode Island School of Design since 1986. She designs and directs a comprehensive planning and evaluation program for the college and the college's museum of art and coordinates the planning process with operational budgets. She also conducts research on students, faculty, and external audiences to support longitudinal, applied assessment, comparative, and accreditation research and reporting. In 1990, Billups cowrote "Integrating Institutional Research Into the Organization," which appeared in Jossey Bass's *Organizing Effective Institutional Research Offices*. She is a member of the American Association of Higher Education, the Society for College and University Planning, the Association for Institutional Research, and cofounder of the Rhode Island Association for Institutional Research. Billups received her Ed.D. from the Peabody College of Vanderbilt University in higher education administration; an M.A. from Rhode Island College in higher education and management; a certificate of arts administration from the University of Rhode Island; and a B.A. from Tufts University in art history.

John A. Dunn, Jr., M.Ed., is Past President of Dean College in Franklin, Massachusetts, a primarily residential transfer-oriented two-year college of 1,000 full-time and 1,400 part-time students. Previously, he was Executive Director of the Center for Planning Information at Tufts University, where he created, developed, and managed a 501(c)3 not-for-profit educational service corporation. Two of Dunn's recent publications include: "Long-Term Tuition Policy: What Happens When Tuition Rises Faster Than Ability to Pay," published by the Association of Governing Boards of Colleges and Universities as Occasional Paper #17; and "An Executive Information System for Fundraising: What Are the Questions?" which he cowrote for *Developing Executive Information Systems for Higher Education*. He is a member of the National Association of Independent Colleges and Universities, the Association of Independent College and Universities in Massachusetts, the Southeastern Association of Colleges of Higher Education in Massachusetts, the Society for College and University Planning, and the Association for Institutional Research, among others. He has consulted for 16 colleges and state task forces. Dunn received his M.Ed. from Harvard University and his B.A. from Wesleyan University in French literature.

K. Scott Hughes, M.S., is President of K. Scott Hughes Associates, a management consulting firm serving postsecondary education institutions located in Mill Valley, California. The firm conducts studies that help clients improve quality service to constituents, increase productivity, and strengthen management's ability to make and execute more informed decisions. Hughes has written several publications on the field of management in education, including: *Years of Challenge, Managing Change in Higher Education*, and *Ratio Analysis in Higher Education*. He is a member of the Licensing Executives Society, the National Association of College and University Business Officers, and the Western Association of College and University Business Officers. Hughes received his M.S. from the University of Illinois in accountancy science. Illinois also granted him a B.S. in accountancy.

G. Gregory Lozier, D.Ed., has been Executive Director of Planning and Analysis at The Pennsylvania State University since 1983. He advises the Office of the President on the continuing development and implementation of Penn State's strategic planning process and oversees staff and analytical support to the study of university policy issues. Lozier also has been a consultant on the topics of strategic planning, collective bargaining, total quality management, and program evaluation for institutions such as Weber State University, the State University of New York at Oswego, Fayetteville State University, the Universidad Autonoma de Guadalajara in Mexico, the Auckland Institute of Technology in New Zealand, and the University of Ghana. He has authored or coauthored over 30 journal articles, book chapters, and monographs. Lozier is a member of the American Association for Higher Education, the Association for the Study of Higher Education, the Association for Institutional Research, the Society for College and University Planning, the American Society for Quality Control, and the European Association for Institutional Research. He received his D.Ed. from The Pennsylvania State University in higher education; his M.S. from Southern Illinois University in education with a concentration in college student personnel work; and his B.A. from Rutgers, The State University of New Jersey in history.

James H. Manifold, M.B.A., C.P.A., is Vice President of Business Affairs/CFO at Scripps College in Claremont, California. He is responsible for financial planning, budgeting, accounting, investments, campus planning, construction management, campus maintenance, and nonacademic personnel. Manifold also is a visiting lecturer at the Peter F. Drucker Management Center of the Claremont Graduate School. In 1992, he wrote "Pay Up Now, or Pay Up Later," an article about funding depreciation, which appeared in *AGB Reports (Trusteeship)*. Manifold is a member of the American Institute of Certified Public Accountants, the National Association of College and University Business Officers, the Society of College and University Planning, and the Los Angeles Higher Education Roundtable. He received his M.B.A. from Rutgers University Graduate School of Business in accounting and his B.S. from Georgetown University's School of Foreign Service. He is a Certified Public Accountant in California and Hawaii.

Deborah J. Teeter, M.B.A., is Director of the Office of Institutional Research and Planning at the University of Kansas. She manages, directs, and coordinates projects; as well as gathers, analyzes, and interprets financial and salary studies; prepares policy and position papers; builds planning models; and consults with Board of Regents staff regarding studies on state financing, faculty activities, program and mission review, among others. Teeter also presents workshops on Total Quality Management (TQM) and consults on topics of TQM, program evaluation, and peer institution selection. Consultancies include Christchurch Polytechnic Institute in New Zealand, Texas A&M University, and the University of Washington. Teeter has published more than 15 journal articles, book chapters, and monographs. Teeter received her M.B.A. from the University of Kansas. She also received her B.S. in business with a concentration in accounting from Kansas.

Robert M. Wilson, M.L.A., is Vice President Emeritus of The Johns Hopkins University and a former consultant to A. Foster Higgins & Co., Inc., a national employee benefits consulting organization based in New York city. He consulted frequently with campus administrators and advised principals and client managers of the firm on college and university faculty and staff benefit issues. Wilson is an honorary life member of the College and University Personnel Association; he has been a member of the American Council of Education and the National Association of College and University Business Officers, among other organizations. He received his M.L.A. from The Johns Hopkins University in the history of ideas and his B.S. from Brown University in mechanical engineering.

Publications and Research Advisory Board 1995-96

1

What Is Strategic Planning?

G. Gregory Lozier

From basic management texts[1] to popular literature,[2] the human resource practitioner interested in initiating a strategic planning process has recourse to hundreds of books, articles, and journals to describe the essential elements of strategic planning. Yet, deciding which resource documents to read and whose step–by–step process to follow can be a daunting exercise for the professional caught up in the day–to–day operations of a human resource office.

The task can be no less challenging to those who call themselves planning professionals. The study of strategic planning is a massive undertaking. Where does one begin? And what definitions should be adopted? The goal of this chapter is to give the reader a common frame of reference with respect to strategic planning—to separate the chaff from the strategic planning literature, to uncover the fundamentals and present them in terms with which the lay person and the planning professional can be equally comfortable. It is also important to recognize what this chapter is not. It is not a cookbook whereby the executive or administrator seeking to initiate a strategic planning process identifies all the necessary ingredients and combines them in the appropriate order to produce the perfect plan. As any chef will attest, great cooking, like strategic planning, requires practice and experimentation with both the ingredients and the process. It takes time and experience to learn what flavors blend best together, when to raise or lower the heat, when additional time will enhance the outcome, and even when to throw something out and start over again.

Defining Strategic Planning

In a more formal, academic treatise on strategic planning, care should be given to the distinctions among definitions of strategy, planning, strategic planning, strategic management, and other terms in this evolving theory of management. For the moment, however, I offer an array of definitions without tying them to a particular term so that we might explore the interconnectedness of the various facets of planning by looking at the array of definitions for the common threads rather than the differences. The section that follows provides a discussion of the key concepts that emerge from these definitions.

Definitions Relating to Planning

— "A participative way of dealing with a set of interrelated problems when it is believed that unless something is done, a desirable future is not likely to occur; and that if appropriate action is taken the likelihood of such a future can be increased."[3]

— "To gain...a sustainable edge over [one's] competitors."[4]

— "Research and other actions needed for the elaboration of a complex set of decisions designed to achieve the goals of an organization....[It involves] data acquisition, goal definition, and the study of alternative means to these goals."[5]

— "The process by which an organization envisions its future and develops the necessary procedures and operations to achieve that future."[6]

— "A systematic way to manage change and create the best possible future."[7]

— "Understand the environment, define organizational goals, identify options, make and implement decisions, and evaluate performance."[8]

— "The essence…is decision making."[9]

— "A disciplined effort to produce fundamental decisions and actions that shape and guide what an organization…is, what it does, and why it does it."[10]

Key Concepts

One can quickly become baffled by the many definitions. However, from these definitions at least five key concepts emerge: process; future; assessment; alternative strategies; and decisions. These concepts are summarized in Table 1.

Table 1

Key Planning Concepts

Process	Design the plan to be systematic and dynamic
Future	Provide a view of where the institution wishes to go
Assessment	Understand the current status
Alternative Strategies	Develop a range of options to achieve established goals
Decisions	Establish the link between goals and strategies and resource allocations

Process. A process is a system of work; it is how things get done. In the case of strategic planning, explicit steps are followed, interactions occur among people and groups, materials are collected, multiple views are presented and collected, plans are drafted and reviewed, and actions are initiated. It is critical that considerable attention be given to the design of the process of planning, both prior to the initiation of a process and throughout its implementation. The process needs to be flexible and dynamic, and responsive to changes in personnel, structure, external forces, and feedback from those participating in its implementation. There are many formal and informal reports on strategic planning processes at colleges and universities that indicate the interactions achieved through the planning process greatly enhanced intracampus communications and general awareness about planning issues. In some instances, presidents report that such interactions were the major achievement of the planning process. A note of caution: although the planning process is a critical component of successful strategic planning, it should be regarded as a necessary but not sufficient element.

Future. Strategic planning provides a college or university, or a department within the institution, a view of where the school wishes to go. It is a view of the future of the institution. Employees must know where the college or university wishes to go to make decisions that will maintain its course.

Assessment. Although the purpose is to identify a future state, it is extremely difficult to devise strategies to get there without thoroughly knowing the current status. Employees need to develop an understanding of the who, what, why, and where the institution is today. Values, beliefs, a sense of purpose, and preexisting conditions and activities provide the foundation from which a future is constructed. They also can be the elements from which employees must disconnect if the preferred future is to be achieved.

Alternative Strategies. After a thorough assessment of the current state of affairs has been conducted and a future state identified, the process should provide an opportunity to generate and consider a full range of goals that might be adopted for creating that future, along with the alternative strategies for achieving those goals. It is important to identify, assess, and record all alternatives, as often a goal or strategy that might not be realistic under current conditions could become extremely viable as other circumstances, either internal or external to the institution, change. A serious pitfall to be avoided is beginning a strategic planning process with a preconceived and inflexible notion of goals and strategies. Typically, many participants are eager to provide everyone with their solutions for the institution, and are glad they finally have been asked. Ownership of the process can help avert such premature judgments.

Decisions. The bottom line for successful strategic planning is to establish the link between the goals and strategies adopted

---

The bottom line for successful strategic planning is to establish the link between the goals and strategies adopted and the decision–making process.

and the decision–making process. Decision making is the key concept on which many processes falter and subsequently fail. For strategic planning to achieve its potential, this element must be built into the design of the strategic planning process at the outset.

Planning Typologies

With these fundamental concepts in hand, it is important to examine briefly several different types of planning, including strategic planning, long-range planning, tactical planning, and operational planning.

Strategic planning. Perhaps the most distinctive feature of strategic planning is its external orientation. While colleges and universities have developed master plans for years, few adequately incorporated a realistic interface with the external environment. Effective strategic planning requires (a) scanning demographic, social, economic, technological, and political trends and (b) assessing their likely impact and the magnitude of such impact on the institution. The scanning effort can be formal (highly structured), informal (unstructured), or both. But without some type of scanning effort, the planning is unlikely to be very strategic.

Strategic planning also is focused broadly; it spans the full boundaries of the organization, sets institutional direction, and identifies the critical issues confronting the institution. Some critical issues have a short-time fuse before acting on the institution, while others are much more long term in nature. As a result, the time frame for strategic planning varies. In a highly volatile, changing environment, a one-year or even a six-month strategic plan may be appropriate and needed. More typically, units think in terms of three- to five-year strategic plans.

Long-Range Planning. Few institutions today prepare documents labeled "long-range plan." Although in disuse because of the insular and linear nature of such planning historically, it is important to recognize that most strategic planning processes have built into them a long-range component. It is the long-range plan that provides the foundation on which strategic planning can function. The long-range plan has a much more expansive time horizon of 10, 15, or even 20 years. And although within that time span much will change to modify the long-term outcome, it declares that the organization will be something different, something more, than it is at present.

Tactical Planning. With a long-term view, an appraisal of the external forces at work on the institution, and the identification of the critical issues at hand, the organization is ready to consider and implement the means to achieve its strategic plans, i.e., design how to get there. Tactical planning is intra-institutional focused and according to Peterson (1989), involves the development of a variety of functional plans, (e.g., an enrollment plan, a facilities plan, or a faculty development plan).[11] It is in the tactical planning stage that the resource implications of proposed strategies need to be explored in depth, i.e., the development of a resource plan.

Operational Planning. Operational planning identifies the institutional procedures to implement the tactical plans. It is the nuts and bolts, day-to-day activities that collectively allow us ultimately to achieve our strategic and long-term plans. Annual budget development and resource allocations are an aspect of operational planning.

Application to Human Resources. An understanding of these planning typologies might be enhanced by considering them in the context of a planning process for an office of human resources. As part of strategic planning, the office might consider issues such as high competition for data processing personnel, escalating health care costs, limited promotion opportunities institution wide, or reallocating personnel displaced by program closures. The office's long-range plan might call for greater integration or merger of the academic and non-academic personnel management functions. Tactical planning could involve the creation of a staff development plan, an information systems plan, or a recruitment and hiring plan. The operational plan would be the establishment and implementation of the procedures necessary to carry out the tactical plans, e.g., training, rewriting policies, preparing correspondence, and carrying out a marketing program.

In its simplest form, planning is involved in answering two fundamental questions: (1) Where does the organization want to go? and (2) How is it going to get there?

Stages of Strategic Planning

Exhibit 1 outlines the basic stages of strategic planning. A brief discussion of each stage and its components follows.

Exhibit 1

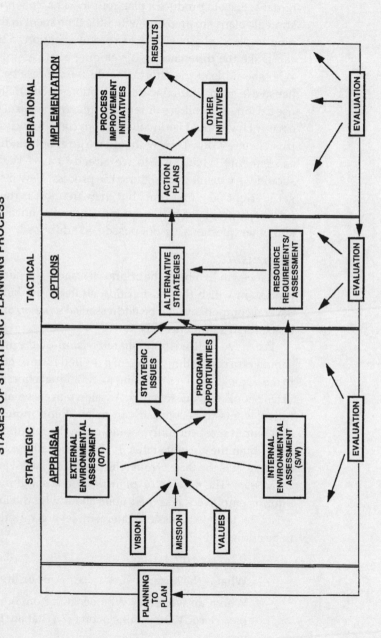

STAGES OF STRATEGIC PLANNING PROCESS

Planning to Plan

Under pressure by central administration or by some external agency to produce a plan four months from now, many strategic plans are prepared with little time spent in the "planning-to-plan" phase. However, careful attention to this stage can make the difference in developing a successful process. Who should lead the effort? Should the process be comprehensive (e.g., institution wide or function specific)? Should we use existing committees or is a new governance structure necessary? How should we involve various constituencies? Should trustees be involved? How should we go about conducting an assessment? What data do we already have? With whom should we consult in designing the process? Few institutions get it "right" the first time, but they are most certain to run into major problems both substantively and politically if these and other questions are not posed and addressed.

Appraisal

As seen in Exhibit 1, the appraisal stage is the period in the process in which the most critical strategic thinking occurs. Several components can be addressed *ad seriatim*, or they can be explored simultaneously.

Vision. A well-written, shared vision of the institution should be a compelling image of a desired future state unique to the school that gives meaning to individual effort and motivates people to work together. A vision reflects what the institution wants to become. It can mean doing more or being different. It most certainly should mean the intention is to be better than the current status. It should be fairly explicit and concrete. It is the target from which to work backward.

Mission. The mission of an institution is about purpose. It informs employees and the public about why the institution exists. To develop a mission statement, several questions need to be addressed.

— Who are we?

— What is the business or service of our institution?

— Whom do we serve? Who benefits from our product or service? Who is our customer? What are his or her needs?

— How do we provide these services? What are the activities and functions performed?

— How are those services distinct from those provided by similar institutions? What are the institution's unique contributions?

Both mission and vision statements should be succinct. However, the typical college or university mission statement reads more like a litany of the institution's historical activities and achievements than a concise statement of purpose. Consider the following mission statement for Otis Elevator: "Moving people and material vertically and horizontally over relatively short distances." This statement provides a marvelous visual image that conveys clearly the precise nature of the business ("over relatively short distances" tells us they are not in the airlines industry).

Similarly, consider the following visions:

— "Land of milk and honey."—Moses

— "...life, liberty and the pursuit of happiness."—Thomas Jefferson

— "Ask not what your country can do for you..."—John F. Kennedy

— "Go fast computers."—Cray Computer

— "When it absolutely, positively has to be there overnight."—Federal Express

— "Democratize the automobile."—Henry Ford

These are more than slogans. They define a future state to which everyone aspires and to which everyone can apply energy and resources.

It is important that many individuals and constituencies be participants in the discussions about mission and vision. At some point it becomes necessary to agree on the key components of each statement, but some compromise is usually necessary to create the final language. Typically, such statements cannot be written effectively by committee. Also, although the development or reconsideration of the institution's or department's mission and vision statements need to be addressed during the appraisal stage of the planning process, it may not be feasible to finalize those statements until one full cycle of planning is complete. Keep in mind that the process, and its products, must be dynamic.

Values. Institutions are not without values. Values express what those people who affiliate with an institution believe in. Statements about values reflect the climate within which employees work and play. They say something about how employees respect one another as individuals and as partners in a larger venture. Strategic planning provides an opportunity to revisit and state these underlying principles. Examples of values that employees might share could include the value of individual creativity and intellectual distinction balanced by the values of the contributions of all cultures to the panorama of human understanding.

It has been said that a mission or purpose without vision has no sense of appropriate scale and that a vision without purpose is just a good idea. It might be added that a mission and vision without values has no legitimacy.

External Assessment of Opportunities and Threats. The earlier discussion of planning typologies identifies the attention given to developing an understanding of the environmental context within which the institution works as one of the most distinguishing characteristics of strategic planning. For an entire college or university, the assessment could cover local, state, regional, national, and international factors and trends. For a department within the college or university, it could also include factors external to the department, but within the institution.

The purpose of the external assessment is to identify external opportunities and threats ...that can influence the future direction of the institution or department.

The purpose of the external assessment is to identify external opportunities and threats (some prefer the notion of constraints) that can influence the future direction of the organization or department. The assessment should consider economic, demographic, political, sociological, technological, scientific, labor market, structural, and competitive trends. The objective is not to presume to make accurate predictions of every variable, but to anticipate possible trends and to use that information to improve the ability to influence the ultimate outcome. The assessment of any one factor may not produce anything regarded as particularly new. In combination, however, new insights about issues and previously unrecognized opportunities may emerge. Not all trends are of equal importance. Some have greater bearing on the institution or a particular department. Others, although feasible alternatives, have a lesser likelihood of materializing. Hence, it is important to consider the potential effect of any particular trend and to prioritize those of greater potential bearing as either an opportunity or a threat.

Internal Assessment of Strengths and Weaknesses. An appraisal of an institution's or a planning group's internal strengths and weaknesses provides an assessment of what the group can or cannot do in quality fashion. It reports on the status of its human, financial, and physical resources relative to the programs and services offered and identifies established limitations as well as internal capabilities. Reviews should consider measures of program cost and productivity as well as indicators of the quality of output programs or services. Where feasible, quantitative measures should be developed and reported. In many instances, it will be necessary to make qualitative judgments— these can be both difficult to make and to report. Too frequently, internal assessments sound more like public relations documents than true assessments. Strong programs and strong staff are prevalent, but inadequate resources provided by some higher level of authority constitute a significant weakness. Certainly, care must be taken in how the internal assessment is written so as not to assign blame to individuals for identified weaknesses. However, a recognition of weaknesses is essential in identifying areas to be addressed or barriers to be overcome in pursuing the organization's strategic goals.

Together, the internal and external assessments of the organization's strengths, weaknesses, opportunities, and threats commonly are referred to as a SWOT analysis. In an initial round of strategic planning it is advisable to conduct a reasonably comprehensive assessment. In subsequent reviews, more limited updates might be in order, in which the analysis focuses on those trends that are most volatile or that have greatest bearing on the unit or institution. Most important, recognize that the assessment is really continuous, as the environment, both external and internal, is dynamic, and changes in that environment can alter strategic goals, tactics, and operations.

Program Opportunities. Strategic program opportunities emerge when the appraisals of the external and internal environments are blended with an institution's or unit's vision, mission, and values. This process establishes the framework for relating elements of program quality and need, and is essential for identifying areas that are candidates for enhancement or areas in which new initiatives should be taken. This time is a real opportunity for participants in the planning process to blue sky "what-if" scenarios and to put forth their boldest dreams, constrained at this stage of the discussion only by the SWOT analysis and the relationship of the dreams to the mission and vision of the unit. That last condition is critical. Beware of those who look to the strategic planning process as the means to put forth every change imaginable or proposals for new programs that have long been on their personal agenda but have no or little support from the rest of the appraisal process.

Strategic Issues. An alternative approach at this stage of the appraisal process is to identify the strategic issues that emerge from a matching of the environmental assessments with the institution's mission, vision, and values. Strategic issues are those fundamental policy questions that an organization must address to achieve a desired future state.[12] Examples of institution-wide strategic issues might be:

— What policies should we initiate to develop and re-
    tain the best faculty?

— How do we respond to increased student interest in
    professional fields and declining interest in the liberal
    arts and sciences?

— With limited new resources, on what basis should pro-
    grams be identified for special enhancement funding?

— How can we provide needed facilities and space in
    response to growing enrollments and increased re-
    search funding in the absence of additional resources
    to create new facilities?

Examples of strategic issues that might be raised by a human resource office include:

— How do we develop a human resource information
    system that equally serves both analytical and opera-
    tional demands?

— What incentives can be developed for limiting the
    growth in worker compensation expenditures?

— What policy changes are needed to accommodate the
    promotion opportunities of current employees and the
    need to create employment opportunities for
    underrepresented constituencies?

Whether exploring program opportunities or identifying strategic issues, at this point of the strategic planning process, it is time for the organization to propose a number of strategic goals that it wishes to pursue over the period of its strategic plan, typically three to five years as noted earlier. Not every goal or strategic issue can be addressed equally. Priorities must be established. By virtue of the appraisal, some issues and goals are more strategic than others. By attempting to respond to too many strategic issues or establish too many "top priority" goals, the institution or department is setting itself up for frustration.

By attempting to respond to too many strategic issues or establish too many "top priority" goals, the institution or department is setting itself up for frustration.

Developing Options

The establishment of a limited number of strategic goals is the transition point from strategic to tactical planning. At this stage of the process, the institution or unit begins to examine the alternative strategies for achieving the goals or for answering the highest priority strategic issues. Initially, many strategies should be identified and considered. But not all options are equally viable. Many barriers impede the implementation of each strategy, the most frequent of which is inadequate resources. Hence, the diagram in Exhibit 1 draws special attention to the need to provide an assessment of all resource requirements for each alternative strategy proposed. Resources are not just financial, but include human resources, facilities, and equipment as well. Barriers other than resources exist, including politics, competitive disadvantage, and uncommitted personnel.

The existence of a barrier does not in and of itself mean the alternative should be discarded. Rather, the next step requires that the discussion consider measures to overcome the barriers. Identification of these tactics ultimately points to the particular options with the greatest possibilities to achieve the desired goals.

Consider the strategic goals adopted by one institution's response to the "increased student interest in professional majors" issue cited earlier. Three strategic goals were adopted: (1) to retain in the institution all qualified students; (2) to maintain enrollment balance across disciplines; and (3) to enhance program quality. A variety of options were raised, e.g., reducing the number of faculty in the liberal arts, reallocating positions and funds, and reducing the number of students admitted to the professional disciplines. Among the respective barriers to these options were the need to retain and support certain core liberal arts programs, the existence of many tenured faculty in the liberal arts, the risk of losing prospective professional–bound students, and the prospect of negative public relations with stakeholders, including parents, students, and legislators. Ultimately, a number of strategies were adopted through consideration of multiple alternatives and the barriers of each. These included: (1) institution of junior year administrative enrollment controls on selected professional programs; (2) implementation of a tuition equipment surcharge for certain technical programs; (3) provision of new resources for some of the high demand fields; (4) development of alumni career days in the liberal arts; and (5) discontinuance and realignment of several programs and departments in the liberal arts. Addressing the issue required that strategies be implemented at many levels, including the program, department, school, college, or university.

Implementation

Action Plans. The implementation stage of planning translates the goals and strategies of the conceptual plan into specific activities. At least two approaches can be pursued, one focusing on initiating process improvements related to the strategy, and one in which the action plans develop other initiatives tied directly to the ongoing operations of the unit.

Process Improvement Initiatives. One means to develop action plans is to identify the processes that support the strategy adopted and then initiate a thorough review of that process with the specific objective of modifying and improving it in ways that will move the institution closer to its targeted goals. This review involves reassessing the basic purpose of the process, identifying process stakeholders and customers, mapping the process and collecting pertinent data to improve understanding of how the process functions and performs, instituting systematic changes to the process, and monitoring their effect on the desired goals. This methodology is covered in more detail in Chapter 7 in which Teeter and Lozier discuss the key conceptual components of Total Quality Management and explore the linkages to strategic planning. At this point, it is important to emphasize that the focus on processes is based on the premise that processes are the means by which things are done. It is a logical extension of this premise, therefore, that changes to existing processes or the design of new processes to implement certain strategies and overcoming barriers are the means toward goal achievement.

In the previous illustration in which strategic goals and strategies for addressing the issue of increased student interest in professional majors are presented, processes that relate to the institution's ability to respond include, for example, advisement, development of degree audit procedures and information systems, the budget allocation process, administration of the alumni career days program, and procedures to reassign faculty and staff displaced by program eliminations and closures to other departments within the institution.

Other Initiatives. In the more traditional approach to the development of action plans, implementation is composed of four essential elements: specification of short-term objectives; development of specific action plans; determination of the responsible office or individual; and identification of resource requirements. The short-term objectives should be stated in measurable terms, so it is easier to determine whether the objective has been realized. Measurable need not be synonymous with quantifiable. However, the statement of the objective should be precise enough to allow an appraisal of the degree of attainment.

Multiple activities may be necessary to achieve the desired objectives. These activities are the unit's specific action plans. These plans should indicate clearly which individuals or offices have responsibility for conducting which activities. Those same individuals or offices should be held accountable periodically for reporting on progress in reaching the stated objectives. Finally, fairly explicit resource requirements need to be established and the likely sources identified. As appropriate, the development of action plans should be tied to the institution's or unit's annual budget development cycle.

Results

In the formative section of this chapter it was observed that the quintessential conceptual element of strategic planning was the necessity to use the strategic planning process to lead the organization to decisions. Assuming that the model has, in fact, induced the making of strategic choices about what the institution's strategic issues are and how they should be addressed, it is equally imperative to monitor for results.

Monitoring is accomplished through systematic and continuous evaluation.

Evaluation

Diagrams of strategic planning stages typically show evaluation as the last, or concluding, stage of the process. In Exhibit 1, evaluation is portrayed as transcending the entire process. Not only is it necessary to determine progress in meeting the objectives of the action plans and, in turn, progress toward achieving the broader strategic goals, all aspects of the process also can be seen as undergoing continuous evaluation. Faculty and staff function in a dynamic environment in which change occurs all around them. When evaluations indicate that a change in either the external or internal environment has occurred, depending on the scope and significance of the change, it could warrant a modification in goals or strategies. Again citing the earlier example of more students pursuing professional education, changing opportunities for graduates in the liberal arts, shifts in the price of technology, the opening of new, competing programs in other institutions, or a shift in the market for faculty members in a particular field from a seller's to a buyer's market, all could have implications for the manner in which the institution should respond.

Faculty and staff function in a dynamic environment in which change occurs all around them.

As part of the evaluation, some form of an annual accounting of progress should be built into the budgeting cycle. Although those responsible quickly get weary if the process requires the same level of intensity to carry out the planning process year after year, some form of annual update tied to resource allocations should be required to ensure continuity and focus on priorities.

You Learn As You Go!

Writing several years ago for the Association of Institutional Research (Dooris and Lozier, 1989), my colleague, Mike Dooris, and I observed that the concept of strategic management emerged from the business literature in the 1970s.[13] This concept has been defined as a "management process or system that links strategic planning and decision making with the day-to-day business of operational management."[14] It is this type of decision-making that Keller advocated in his book *Academic Strategy* (1983) subtitled "The Management Revolution in

Higher Education." But strategic management in both corporate and higher education settings became the target of a number of criticisms and by the middle of the 1980s, the staying power of strategic management was coming into question.[15] Toward the end of the decade, a number of studies emerged that tested whether strategic planning made a difference in higher education.

In their review of planning experiences at a sample of institutions across the United States, Schmidtlein and Milton (1988) concluded that there is a considerable gap between the strategic planning literature's often optimistic prescriptions about formal planning processes and the cynicism, resistance, and confusion that often accompanies campus planning.[16] Another 1988 study, by Meredith, Lenning, and Cope of 34 research institutions, concluded that institutions that had engaged in what respondents classified as "bona fide" strategic planning reported greater satisfaction with the effort and a belief that they were achieving better results than counterparts who could not characterize their institution's efforts as bona fide planning.[17] Both reports suggest participant satisfaction may depend not as much on *whether* strategic planning is undertaken, but on *how*. "The problems often found with strategic planning applications—over-fragmentation, paper driven, control oriented, mechanistic and modeling dependent, and failure to account for organizational culture and constituency groups—are more the result of how we apply strategic planning principles than with the basic constructs themselves."[18] (Gilmore and Lozier, 1987) It is not surprising, therefore, to read Schmidtlen and Milton's report that one president who had spoken at length about the major benefits of planning in his institution concluded, when asked about repeating the process, "'Never during the remainder of my tenure as president.'"[19] It also would not be surprising that this institution did not derive the benefits of another institution that persisted over several years, as reported by Clugston in yet another study.[20] Reporting on how strategic planning affected resource allocation decisions in a research institution, the study's regression results showed small but significant effects, in which strategic priorities explained about 3 percent of the variation in budget allocations to departments. The study concluded that strategic planning did make a difference.

Participant satisfaction may depend not as much on whether strategic planning is undertaken, but on how.

And what was the "difference" between this institution and that of the previously quoted president? Recognition that most of the change realized through strategic planning depends more on gradualism than dramatic shifts. One author (Quinn, 1980) combined theory drawn from business and government to make a convincing case for "logical incrementalism."[21] In brief, Quinn argues that successful management is often tentative, gradual, flexible, open to feedback and change, and adaptive. For that reason, Quinn believes major changes in strategy should be allowed to emerge and evolve over time. Mintzberg and Waters (1984) have even distinguished between deliberate and emergent strategies, in which emergent strategies are those realized despite, or in the absence of, intentions.[22]

Scott (1981, p. 281) makes a similar point about the importance of permitting "experiential learning"—the idea that while managers start out with broad goals, those goals (along with strategies to achieve them) must be allowed to be shaped and modified in response to environmental feedback.[23] Similarly, Hayes (1985) expanding on an idea of Brilker, notes that a strategic manager is much like a traveler lost in a swamp with a constantly changing topography.[24] In contrast to the traveler going from point A to point B on an interstate highway, much as a long–range plan might set out to do, the traveler in the swamp is better served by a compass (strategic plan) that indicates the general direction to follow and that allows the traveler to pursue unique opportunities and overcome unexpected obstacles, including cypress stumps, water moccasins, and deep water during the course of the journey.

This chapter does not offer the human resource professional a fail–safe recipe for successful strategic planning. There is a great deal of terminology with which to become familiar; important differences to internalize regarding strategy, strategic planning, and strategic management; governance issues to address; and commitment from the HR professional, those to whom the HR professional reports, and those who report to him or her. Will it make a difference? It can, if the human resource practitioner is willing to learn by doing.

Notes

1. Pennings, J. M. et al. 1985. *Organizational Strategy and Change.* San Francisco: Jossey-Bass Publishers.

2. Blanchard, K. and S. Johnson. 1982. *The One-Minute Manager.* New York: Morrow.

3. Ackoff, R. L. 1981. *Creating the Corporate Future: Plan or Be Planned For.* New York: John Wiley & Sons, p. 52.

4. Ohmae, K. 1982. *The Mind of the Strategist: The Art of Japanese Business.* New York: McGraw–Hill Book Co., p. 36.

5. Benveniste, G. 1989. *Mastering the Politics of Planning: Crafting Credible Plans and Policies That Make a Difference.* San Francisco: Jossey–Bass Publishers, p. 19, 21.

6. Goodstein, L. D. et al. 1986. "Applied Strategic Planning: A New Model for Organizational Growth and Vitality." In *Strategic Planning: Selected Readings.*, ed. J. W. Pfeiffer, San Diego, CA: University Associates, Inc., p. 2.

7. Sorkin, D. L. et al. ND. *Strategies for Cities and Counties: A Strategic Planning Guide.* Washington, DC: Public Technology, Inc., p. 1.

8. Morrison, J. L., et al. 1984. *Futures Research and the Strategic Planning Process: Implications for Higher Education.* ASHE–ERIC Higher Education Research Report No. 9, p. 8

9. Keller, G. 1983. *Academic Strategy: The Management Revolution in American Higher Education.* Baltimore, MD: The Johns Hopkins University Press, p. 141.

10. Bryson, J. M. 1988. *Strategic Planning for Public and Nonprofit Organizations: A Guide to Strengthening Organizational Achievement.* San Francisco: Jossey–Bass Publishers, p. 5.

11. Peterson, M. W. 1989. "Analyzing Alternative Approaches to Planning." In P. Jedamus and M. W. Peterson, *Improving Academic Management.* San Francisco: Jossey–Bass Publishers, p. 113–63.

12. Bryson, *Strategic Planning for Public and Nonprofit Organizations.*

13. Dooris, M. J. and G. G. Lozier. 1989. "Can Strategic Management Work in Colleges and Universities?" Paper presented at the 29th Annual Forum of the Association for Institutional Research.

14. Gluck, F. S. et al. 1982. "The Four Phases of Strategic Management." *Journal of Business Strategy,* 2 (3), p. 10; It is this type of rigorous decision making that Keller advocated in *Academic Strategy.*

15. Gray, D. H. 1986. "Uses and Misuses of Strategic Planning." *Harvard Business Review,* 86 (1), p. 89–97.

16. Schmidtlein, F. A. and T. H. Milton. 1988. "Campus Planning in the United States: Perspectives from a Nation-Wide Study." Paper presented at the 10th Annual Forum of the European Association for Institutional Research.

17. Meredith, M. et al. 1988. "After Six Years, Does Strategic Planning Matter?" Paper presented at the 28th Annual Forum of the Association for Institutional Research.

18. Gilmore, J. L. and G. G. Lozier. 1987. "Managing Strategic Planning: A Systems Theory Approach." *Educational Planning*, 6 (1), p. 12–23.

19. Schmidtlein and Milton, "Campus Planning," p. 28.

20. Clugston, R. M. 1988. "Strategic Adaptation in an Organized Anarchy: Priority Setting and Resource Allocation in the Liberal Arts College of a Public Research University." Chicago, IL: American Association of University Administrators Foundation.

21. Quinn, J. B. 1980. *Strategies for Change: Logical Incrementalism.* Homewood, IL: Richard D. Irwin, Inc.

22. Mintzberg, H. and J. A. Waters. 1985. "Of Strategies, Deliberate and Emergent." *Strategic Management Journal*, 6, p. 257–72.

23. Scott, W. R. 1981. *Organizations: Rational, Natural, and Open Systems.* Englewood Cliffs, NJ: Prentice-Hall, Inc., p. 281.

24. Hayes, R. H. 1985. "Strategic Planning—Forward or Reverse?" *Harvard Business Review*, 63 (6), p. 111–19.

2

What Is the Problem You Are Trying to Solve?

John A. Dunn, Jr.

This chapter raises a series of questions a college or university president should think through when considering undertaking a strategic planning process. Most of the questions are based on the reality that the institution is made up of individual human beings who will bring their personal as well as professional hopes and fears to the process. The human resource professional should be in a good position to advise the president on these matters.

Overview

The general outline of strategic planning presented in chapter one summarizes insights gained from the experience at many institutions. This summary does not mean, however, that there is some canned approach to strategic planning that can be applied to every institution, in every situation. The most important questions the president needs to ask before undertaking *any* strategic planning process are: "what is the problem we are trying to solve?" and "where does the college want to get to?" Strategic planning, undertaken as a formalized participatory process, is only one of many tools a president has with which to help an institution move in the desired direction. Formalized planning processes are at least as much political exercises as intellectual ones; the president who wants to start such a process would be well advised to structure it carefully to maximize the probability of achieving a useful outcome.

Planning processes that are undertaken in the absence of a clearly identified problem to solve or a direction to take typically produce large amounts of both paper and frustration.

There are examples of institutions where a broad constituency-based planning process was undertaken without a clear understanding of the nature of the problem or the goal. Perhaps the process was launched because the board chairperson thought the college "ought to have a plan." Perhaps it was because the state coordinating commission required "a plan" from every public institution. Perhaps it was just something the president thought was part of his or her job description. In any case, planning processes that are undertaken in the absence of a clearly identified problem to solve or a direction to take typically produce large amounts of both paper and frustration. They seldom have any significant effect on what actually happens over the next several years, except to undermine the credibility of the sponsors of the process and of any subsequent planning efforts.

Articulation of the Rationale for Planning

The "what destination" and "what problem" questions are overlapping but not identical. Together they are intended to produce a clear articulation of the rationale for engaging in the planning process. Once that rationale is explicit, the president and others can make cogent decisions about the focus and character of the process and about its leadership, breadth of constituency involvement, structure, and timing.

The rationale for engaging in the planning process well may be among those commonly understood as the traditional goals of planning, such as survival of a demographic shift, implementation of a new curriculum, start of a new branch campus, or preparation for a capital campaign. In most cases, the president (and usually the cadre of other senior administrators and key trustees) has a fairly good idea of what the outcome is to be. Part of the purpose for the planning in such circumstances may be to educate the rest of the community as to the need for such a change and to enlist its help in sharpening and enhancing the vision. Nonetheless, the real point here is to figure out how best to implement an already fairly clear objective rather than to alter it materially. The process and staffing for this planning process can then be chosen with those goals in mind.

In other contexts, the president may genuinely seek assistance in thinking about changes in the mission of the institution, in creating a new strategic vision. Even in these cases, he or she is likely to have some preconceptions about which alternatives are desirable and feasible and which ones are not. The planning process in such situations probably should involve a much different cast of characters and a much different approach, at least at the early stages. The task of critical thinking and of imagining alternatives might best start with charges to individuals or small groups to write "think pieces." A series of retreats with small key groups might explore possibilities. Only when some reasonably clear vision has been articulated can the institution's leaders thoughtfully undertake to broaden the process and begin to consider implementation issues.

Sometimes a president will wish to undertake formalized planning for reasons that have more to do with the process itself than with the resulting document—to restore a productive atmosphere and teamwork to a troubled campus; to change the self-image of the institution; to enable a community to recognize its environment has changed and that, while the institution's mission remains the same, its approach must be different. Here again, the process and personnel selected for the planning can be selected more astutely once the purpose is clear.

Finally, there well may be circumstances in which a president may wish to avoid any sort of formal planning process or may wish to delay beginning one. He or she may recognize that certain personnel changes are needed before a planning process could produce results of the sort wanted. Or he or she may be confronted with rapidly changing budget situations in which coherent constructive planning is virtually impossible, as happened in some states in the early 1990s where public institutions had to cope with five or six budget recessions in a six-month period.

Personal Operational Planning Versus Managerial Planning

Planning is an integral part of every administrator's or manager's job, in higher education just as in any other organized activity. Everyone plans every day, just to cope with our lives, personally and professionally. This informal and pervasive planning involves thinking ahead about what needs to be accomplished, what the alternatives are, how to go about it, what tasks are more urgent than others and how to prioritize the time, what resources are available to accomplish the task, etc. Some planning is explicit—talking with colleagues or spouses, writing down the steps and alternatives—more frequently, planning is done mentally, almost intuitively.

In personal and professional lives, people plan because they want or need to accomplish some objective—to change something. People plan to accomplish something that would not occur by itself, or to avoid something that might happen if action is not taken, or because without planning people do not know the best way to proceed in the direction they want.

When people move beyond planning in their own heads to involve others in the process, they introduce another dimension: the process of collaborative planning by itself facilitates and may even become part of the desired result. If a board of trustees is asked to help determine how an institution can raise more money to support its programs, the board's ideas will be helpful; more importantly, the board members themselves become more committed to the goal and are likely to be more active contributors and solicitors. In moving beyond personal in-the-single-head planning to involving others, one begins to move (often very productively) from deciding what to do to beginning to accomplish it.

Herein lies the key difference between planning as an individual, and the collaborative planning that individuals engage in as managers. Management has been defined as achieving results through others. Part of that process often can be aided by involving others in determining what to do and how to do it—and that very involvement often can be helpful in achieving the results intended.

Formalized Planning As One of Many Tools

In a college or university it is occasionally useful to formalize the planning process—to describe a task and to charge a group of individuals with thinking through the issues and making recommendations.

Formalized planning processes have great benefits in shared wisdom and broadened commitment to the solutions, but they have costs and limits. They are expensive in time and effort; they tend to be slow; they deal with questions of expansion far better than with those of contraction or fundamental change; and the plans they produce are likely to be no more visionary or intelligent than the people who make up the committee.

Formalized planning processes are only one of many tools a president has to move the institution in the direction he or she thinks appropriate. The human resource professional can be helpful to a president in identifying the best approach (in part by articulating clearly how the change would be perceived by others at the institution) and in managing it for maximum effect. Among these other approaches are the following:

The human resource professional can be helpful to a president in identifying the best approach...and in managing it for maximum effect.

— Appointing people who share the president's views to key positions. It may well be that the desirable directions are well understood but are not being implemented effectively. If so, the appointment to key positions of one or two people who share the president's ideas and commitment can help.

— Changing the organizational structure to clarify responsibility for achieving the desired results, to give someone the organizational resources to deal with the situation, or to signal to the community a shift in priorities. For instance, if the chief academic officer is to lead the process of institutional change, moving the budget office away from the chief financial officer and into his or her area can give that person the resources and the visibility to accomplish the job as well as the responsibility. Another illustration is to create an enrollment management position to take over responsibility for all admissions, financial aid, retention, and related activities.

— Changing people's job descriptions or titles. A shift in title and responsibilities from vice president for administration to vice president for finance can clarify expectations.

— Providing incentives and disincentives—e.g., promotions, salary increases, better offices, staff assistance, larger budgets—to help people move in the directions indicated. People watch for signals and respond accordingly.

— Allocating additional resources to the desired activities. Although annual budget reallocations are difficult and tend to be only marginal, they can still be important. The deletion of a faculty position in one program and the addition of a position in another has both real and symbolic value.

— And plain old-fashioned jawboning. A president should never underestimate the effect of his or her visible continued attention to an area.

To reiterate the point made earlier: the president should have a clear idea what the reason is for planning (where the institution wants to go, or what the problem is the institution is trying to solve). If a formalized participatory process is the best method to achieve the desired result, it can and should be used. In many circumstances, however, formalized planning proves to be a clumsy weapon—wonderfully powerful for hitting certain targets, but hard to move, difficult to aim, and occasionally explosive.

The levers for change listed earlier are *always* available to the president, whether or not a formalized planning process is chosen. They may be used to help prepare the case for a formalized process; to deal with an issue where a formalized process would not be possible or productive; and to help implement the recommendations coming out of the planning process.

Planning As a Political As Well As an Intellectual Process

The purpose of planning is to change something. Change is threatening. It means giving up something, altering familiar paths. It means venturing into territory in which people feel less comfortable, less competent. Institutions are made up of people; like individuals, institutions change behavior only when it becomes clear the change is necessary to accomplish something of value, or to avoid something feared.

Changing an institution is a *political* process. Deciding what change is needed may be an intellectual process, but accomplishing the change means getting others to support the change, or at least to go along with it. Formalized planning processes sometimes may be helpful in deciding what changes are needed, but they play their most important role in starting the political process of change. By involving a number of people, preferably trustworthy people and opinion leaders, the need for change and the considerations involved become evident to the broader population.

In higher education, it is hard to remember that people rarely change their beliefs and behavior as a result of rational argument. People have been taught to intellectualize, dissect, theorize, and articulate elegantly. They have been taught to avoid emotional appeals. HR professionals know from experience, however, that while it is fairly easy to give someone new and different information, it is much harder to get him or her to act differently on the basis of that information.

Changing beliefs and behavior involves an unfreezing of current sets of ideas and values, a shifting to a different set, then refreezing. The hardest part is helping people unfreeze, to understand with their whole being rather than just with their head why change is needed. Possible approaches include: cognitive dissonance, writing scenarios, focusing long term, and thinking in the concrete.

Creating Cognitive Dissonance. Faculty or staff may be willing to rethink their beliefs if they see their prior views are partial, self-serving, or simply wrong. Planners and institutional researchers can assemble data and projections to help them grasp dangers or opportunities in the trends at the institution or in its environment. Outside speakers can exemplify a different perspective. Even asking people to adopt roles other than their traditional ones in a dramatized problem-solving episode can be eye-opening. Human resource professionals can help faculty and staff members see that treasured institutional procedures are only idiosyncratic and that there are other and perhaps more effective policies or practices in use at other institutions.

Writing Scenarios. It is easy to assume that the future one expects is the only likely future. Writing alternative futures that play out the consequences of different assumptions can prepare one to think more flexibly.

Focusing on Where One Would Like to Be 5 or 10 Years from Now, Rather Than Next Year. Asking people what they would really like the institution to become can help get beyond current "thinking with blinders." Having articulated a vision, one can then begin to ask more usefully what it would take to get from here to there.

Thinking in the Concrete Rather Than the Abstract. Politicians know that people respond to the affecting anecdote and the personal insight far more than to the abstract concept. Asking someone what he or she would like his daily life to be like in a few years may cause much more creative thinking than asking what the institution should be like.

Having "unfrozen" the prior ideas and values, one can then move ahead to thinking about the desired future. Remember that change is frightening. *People need to see in the new and changed future something of benefit to themselves: something of which they can be proud, or a refuge from harm, or at least a role in which they can be comfortable.*

A great many changes have been wrought in institutions in the last few years out of fear—budget cuts, job losses, eroding markets, etc. Formalized planning processes tend not to be helpful in these situations. Members of a planning committee may feel a need to protect their area or may be reluctant to urge cuts in one field, lest they be on the receiving end next time around.

It has been said that there are really only three approaches to downsizing that are guaranteed to produce savings. One is to impose an absolute freeze on hiring. People die, retire, or leave for other jobs. If they are not replaced, the organization shrinks. The problem here, of course, is that the process takes time to work, the reductions are not always in the areas one would choose, and the reductions do not always involve the nonperformers. In fact, it may be the good people who leave. The second tactic is for one person (usually the president or the chief budget officer) to designate arbitrarily which areas are cut and by how much. The third is to appoint a committee to make recommendations, wait until it has proved itself entirely incapable of making cuts, and then have one person arbitrarily designate the areas to be cut and by how much.

If higher education in most areas of the country is now at the bottom of the demographic and economic trough, it now may be possible to plan for things desired instead of things feared. Here, formalized planning committees are generally more productive.

If higher education in most areas of the country is now at the bottom of the demographic and economic trough, it now may be possible to plan for things desired instead of things feared.

Components of a Planning Process

If the president decides to proceed with a formalized planning process, the next step is to structure that process in the way most likely to produce the desired results. There are a number of considerations, including: the charge, the leadership, the membership, the structure, the support, the timetable, the relationship with other institutional decision making, and the desired outcome.

The Charge. Precisely what is it that the planning process is supposed to accomplish? To explore a field? To recommend a single course of action or to present alternatives? To issue think pieces to educate the community? To be the lightning rod or heat shield for the president, so he or she can respond to problems by saying a committee has been appointed to study the situation? To validate the president's chosen direction or to explore new alternatives and strategies?

The Leadership. Should the president or one of his or her immediate lieutenants chair the committee? Or should the task be given to a dean, a faculty leader, or even to a dissident faculty member who might be co-opted? (Sometimes asking the critic to study the situation and recommend viable solutions can be educational for all involved.) Remembering that a planning process is a political instrument, not just an intellectual exercise, what are the signals that the appointment to leadership gives to the rest of the community?

Membership on the Planning Committee. Who else is involved? Only the president's friends and allies, or a balanced group? How are the formal and informal power structures represented? Are professional staff involved, or only faculty? Are other affected groups (clerical, physical plant, etc.) involved? Does the committee have within its membership the expertise needed for the job? For instance, if the task involves making budgetary or financial recommendations, is the chief financial officer included?

Committee Structure. To what extent is the committee free to structure itself? Are there subcommittees on various tasks, or one overall group? If there are subcommittees, what are the signals given depending on who is on the central committee and who is on the task groups? How extensive should community involvement be in the process? Can the committee conduct surveys, hold hearings, or otherwise collect community input?

Support for the Process. What sorts of support are available to the committee? Can it request support from the budget office, institutional research, or the provost's office? Can it talk to people outside the committee, such as board members, outside experts, etc.? Is technical, logistical, or other support made directly available, or does it have to be requested each time? All of these signals are read easily by the community.

The Timetable. What is the target date for completion of the committee's task? Allowing for reflection and study of alternatives and for slow community digestion of possibly unpalatable moves may in some circumstances be desirable, if practical. Under other circumstances, a sense of urgency with forced deadlines may be important to not miss an opportunity or to give everyone involved a sense of the critical importance of the outcome.

The Relationship to the Budget Process and Other Institutional Decision Making. All too often formalized planning processes produce recommendations with academic program implications or budgetary implications that have not been integrated with the ongoing institutional decision-making process. The maxim is that nothing happens if it is not in the budget. The committee and the budget office need to be clear that the recommendations must be tested for budgetary feasibility and that they must be incorporated into the ongoing operational and capital budget processes. There are some circumstances, however, when it may be useful to charge a committee with focusing on long-range goals rather than immediate budget realities. There, the outcomes may be quite independent of current budget processes but may serve as targets toward which they should be oriented in ensuing years.

The Desired Outcome. Precisely what is the committee supposed to produce? A document? A budget plan? A set of provocative think papers? A series of discussions on campus? Materials that can be useful for off-campus audiences, such as community leaders or system office personnel?

If it is considered seriously that the purpose of planning is to change things, and that formalized planning processes are political exercises as much as intellectual exercises, the process needs to be structured to achieve the desired goals. Now it should be even more evident why it is important for the president who creates the planning committee to be clear (at least in his or her own mind) about the purpose for the exercise. That purpose need not necessarily be communicated to anyone else, but if it is clearly understood, the formalized planning process can be made much more useful.

Visions and Plans

In the last few years it has become fashionable to talk about "strategic visions" instead of "strategic plans." The two approaches are based on the importance of the strategic perspective: looking at what happens outside the institution as well as within it and tuning the institution to take advantage of positive developments and to avoid negative developments in that larger world. They differ in their emphasis on imagination and implementation. Strategic visions embody the wisdom of the old adage: "Dream no little dreams: they have no power to move men's minds." They are based on the understanding that change comes about not when a statistic-laden volume is produced but when a new understanding or vision changes the way people act. Strategic plans are based on the recognition that visions may be enticing but the plans may be nothing more than castles in the air until specific achievable goals can be identified and assigned to individuals and teams for implementation.

In reality, of course, both visions and plans are needed. Human beings need to understand where they are trying to go and also how to go about getting there. In the excellent *Guide to New Planners*, Norris and Poulton (1991) advocate the "Lewis and Clark" model in opposition to the "Cook's Tour" one.[1] In other words, it is necessary to identify a clear objective, such as exploring the newly acquired western territory. However, since no one knows in advance all the conditions that will be encountered on changing terrain over an extended period of time, one should not attempt to prescribe in detail just where one will be and just what activities one will be engaged in at each stage.

Human resource professionals can perhaps be most helpful to the president in reminding him or her again and again that the institution is composed of individual human beings.

Getting the Vision Down to All Departments

In developing almost any sort of plan there will be differing ideas and levels of enthusiasm. There almost certainly will be pockets of resistance. Someone is sure to take the point of view that "It's wonderful if everyone else wants to change, but we're doing the right thing now." In fact, he or she may believe that deeply or may find the anticipated changes particularly threatening to his or her field or activity.

This inevitable human reality has to be treated differently in each situation, depending on the individuals involved and the centrality of the issue to the feasibility of the plan. A president has a number of options, including:

— Using the levers identified earlier to help the individuals involved move in the desired directions.

— Talking until vital problems can be aired and addressed in the plan. Taking a step back now and again when resistance is encountered often can permit one to move two steps forward the next time.

— Compromising or including in the plan some element the resistant party finds important.

— Adopting the "what systems will get serviced" approach. In recent years, computing service organizations generally have abandoned trying to tell academicians which machines and operating systems to buy. They have found that it works much better to allow total freedom of purchase, but to let everyone know that only brands X and Y will get user support and service. This approach can be adopted in other areas as well.

Advice to the Human Resource Professional

Human resource professionals can perhaps be most helpful to the president in reminding him or her again and again that the institution is composed of individual human beings. While many may be intellectually brilliant and pedagogically creative, they are still human. The aim of any planning is to achieve some result; that result is going to be achieved by the human beings that make up the organization, and will affect all of them. A human resource professional may be able to help the president select and apply the tools he or she uses (perhaps including formalized strategic planning) to move in the desired directions, since the human resource professional may know better than anyone else how those actions may motivate, scare, or empower the human beings at the institution.

Notes

1. Norris, D. M. and N. L. Poulton. 1991. *A Guide for New Planners.* Ann Arbor, MI: Society for College and University Planning.

3

Begin at the Beginning

Felice D. Billups

After defining and describing strategic planning and justifying why institutions should plan, the next step in this critical institutional process is to identify *how* institutions *begin* the process. This chapter reviews the particulars of planning in an academic environment to ensure an effective outcome.

Planning in Higher Education

Academic culture resembles an "organized anarchy." College and university cultures share the same "ambiguous purpose and multi-faceted goals" that dictate the institutional behavior that confounds a planning process. Since Cohen and March define organized anarchies as cultures where members live within "a normative context that presumes purpose and within an organizational context that denies it," it is not surprising that academic planning tries the most patient soul.[1]

The "garbage can" theory of decision making (Cohen and March, 1974) confirms the concept of anarchy and ambiguity in the campus culture. The authors explain that an institution is "a collection of choices looking for problems, issues and feelings looking for a decision situation."[2] The process of decision making, communication, and planning in an academic setting is much like that "garbage can." As the authors note "A major feature of the garbage can process is the partial coupling of problems and choices. Although we think of decision making as a process for solving problems, that is often not what happens. Problems are worked upon in the context of some choice, but choices are made only when the shifting combinations of problems, solutions, and decision makers happen to make action possible. Quite commonly this is after problems have left a given choice arena or before they have discovered it (decisions by flight or oversight)."[3]

The "garbage can" theory of decision making confirms the concept of anarchy and ambiguity in the campus culture.

Another perspective on collegiate decision making includes the various strata of administration, faculty, and staff as the key internal decision-making groups. One potential explanation for the dysfunctional decision making at institutions can be explained by the *different* styles of decision making exhibited by *different* work groups. Working from Baldridge's (1977) theory of academic decision making, there are four basic models: bureaucratic, collegial, political, and democratic. Add to those categories the theory of anarchy, and the stage is set.[4]

For instance, support staff members usually make their decisions based on the bureaucratic model. They follow the rules, they take orders, they give instructions, and they adhere to a well defined and clear set of agreed on behaviors. A second group, the middle managers, usually respect the collegial model of decision making, since they are caught between the established rules and the nuances of institutional decision making. In other words, they try to make decisions and work with each other while caught between what *should* be done versus what *occurs* based on influence and power. A third group of decision makers, the senior management, reflects the best example of political decision making in action. Every behavior typically is guided by the anticipated outcome, the transfer of power and territory, the visibility of position, and the balance of influence.

This situation is complicated enough, but the models of democracy and anarchy have yet to be introduced. Typically, students behave in a democratic fashion, believing that everyone should be involved in decision making on campus. Conversely, faculty exemplify anarchy in their decision making, enacting a circular and somewhat conflicting behavior pattern. In total, the sum of all these parts makes for a rather creative, chaotic, and ultimately generative (if not frustrating) atmosphere for planning.

To further complicate the decision-making process in academe, the question remains as to why such confused institutions want to plan in the first place. March (1972) proposes that when events or outcomes do not occur as the organization intends, the search for new alternatives begins in earnest.[5] In particular, research reveals that organizations search for new alternatives in the face of constraint, difficult economies, and failing morale. Planning is often introduced in such periods and places the organization at risk for making poor decisions. Hence, a college or university often plans because it does not like the decisions made previously, or more commonly, it does not approve of who made them.

In short, academic planning processes are never based in logic. Since planning processes depend on decision making as the foundational activity, and collegiate decision-making styles tend to the unconventional and nonhierarchical, a challenging climate for strategic planning evolves. As implied by the phrase "organized anarchy," the process of planning in academe is indeed circular and conflicting. As March (1972) suggests decision making and planning are based in "bounded rationality rather than complete rationality."[6]

Given this appalling lack of logic and reason, it is imperative to focus on how best to conduct a planning process by understanding an organization's dynamics. Human resource professionals must encourage colleagues to ask themselves key questions and be aware of the potential pitfalls and challenges. The following review of the planning process will serve as a review of the key components underlying any fledgling planning exercise: history, climate, identity, participation, timing, communication, and implementation. The chapter will conclude with a few words of advice on how to avoid some common planning problems.

Begin with the Past

To effectively begin a planning process there must be awareness of the *types* of planning activities that have occurred previously. How has planning traditionally been conducted institutionally? Who was involved? Who initiated the process? What valuable perspectives can affect the next phase of planning?

At one small private college, planning had never been undertaken as a formal activity until the college reached its centennial anniversary. Historically, decisions were made by senior administrators without input from faculty, students, alumni, or staff. When considering a planning process, it was critical for the institution to begin by holding numerous informal discussion groups (with diverse campus groups) to identify perceptions of the college and its future. In this way a planning process could then be structured that reflected the collective sense of identity shared by the community while ensuring ownership of the process as it proceeded.

Conversely, a large research institution found that planning had become a regular part of campus life ever since the university had merged with a smaller teaching college 10 years earlier. During the ensuing period, planning had been critical to maintain a focused sense of mission and direction and to justify budget allocations during difficult economic times. Planning always had been a painful experience but one where the larger community was involved only minimally after the first few years. Given the nature of the constraints and difficult decisions required, management determined the process was best left to the operational managers. While it may not work best at every institution, there will be occasions where the top administrators should be the only members of the planning team. An organization in flux or unstable may suffer further from a prolonged process of planning and discussion. Sometimes quick decisions and a succinct planning process serve the organization best.

In these two examples, and in countless others, reflecting on past planning efforts, or the lack thereof, remains critical to understanding how to conduct a new process. To ignore the prior cycle of planning efforts negates each successive effort; planning groups need to incorporate the lessons of the past continuously to position the institution for future success.

The Planning Climate

Once a sense of history has been established, the next step is to assess the current organizational climate for planning. How do campus groups perceive planning? Is there resistance to planning as a shared process? How can any feelings of skepticism be overcome? A sensitive assessment of the campus climate, culture, and ethos is critical to any steps undertaken.

One midsize public institution survived a decade of difficult and turbulent times. The administrative staff had unionized, enrollment had declined dramatically, and the gap between faculty and senior administrators had widened to a level of considerable distrust. During those years, the president and her staff had continued an institutional planning process, albeit in an autocratic manner. By the time a new president had assumed leadership and attempted to continue planning, the campus culture was such that a meaningful process was nearly impossible. The new president needed to spend months building relationships and trust with the various campus groups before planning could even be discussed again. Further, the president's intent was to involve the entire institution in a democratic planning effort, which differed from prior history. Much fence building and constant informal discussion needed to occur before any formalized process could resume.

Developing a sense of community and institutional self-awareness remains essential to a good planning process.

An institution that has never engaged in a planning process (one of the select few that has not yet done so) possesses a clean slate of enthusiasm and energy with which to work. Nonetheless, the planning team and planning coordinator must communicate clearly, from the beginning, their aspirations and desires to involve numerous groups of people. While time and energy may not be spent correcting the problems of the past, the basic rules of good group behavior still need to be observed.

A Sense of Self

Developing a sense of community and institutional self-awareness remains essential to a good planning process. Many methods and exercises exist to help a campus focus on identity and institutional image. Devices such as survey questionnaires, focus groups, small group retreats, workshops, and seminars all contribute to developing a sense of ethos and community.

There are many ways to encourage a campus of diverse individuals to build a community and encourage dialogue. Many institutions find it useful to hire consultants or facilitators to run workshops or retreats to discuss institutional values and goals. Often these group sessions are preceded by a survey questionnaire that asks respondents to identify the institution's strengths and weaknesses. In addition, surveying faculty, staff, and student populations with a mix of focus groups and survey questionnaires is a good way to gather feedback. Presenting the results of the research usually provides a forum for discussion and further community building.

Involvement of Groups and Individuals

Which groups or individuals should be involved in the planning process and in what ways? How do internal group participants differ from external group participants? What should be the extent of trustee involvement? Is a consultant needed?

People and Programs. Critical program directors must be involved in any planning process, including (but not be limited to): academic affairs, financial affairs, enrollment management, institutional advancement, student life programs, academic support, administrative affairs, human resources, equipment and technology, auxiliaries, and physical plant. Any one of these areas, if excluded from a planning process, can negate the work of the process overall. As internal group members, these individuals have an active stake in the outcome of the planning process. While they remain central to the process, they must be balanced by some important "external" groups, specifically including trustees and alumni.

Trustees. Trustees should be involved in planning in a special way. As overseers, they need to be apprised of the general directions and objectives for the institution's future, but they do not need to be involved in the details of the process. Regular sessions, two or three times a year, between the president and the board, provide adequate forums for discussion about institutional planning, while still leaving the mechanics of the process to the planning team.

The Role of Human Resources. One of the most critical planning questions to ask is the question of future staffing. All too often, colleges and universities conduct planning processes exclusively from the academic program perspective and never take into account that staff planning is a necessary component. A projection of the human resources of the institution must be conducted and integrated into the institutional plan carefully.

How does a campus typically react to human resource involvement in planning? Many academic environments distrust the human resource function, seeing it as superfluous and too businesslike. In fact, almost everything that happens in any organization (and more so in a college or university) is rooted in human relationships and human endeavors. Promoting the involvement of the human resource professional in the planning process is key. To dispel any discomfort with that involvement, the human resource staff must be well integrated into every facet of planning. When the human resource professional plays an active and visible role in planning, it enhances the credibility of the process overall.

Consultation and Consultants. Is a consultant needed? All institutions struggle with this issue. Ultimately, the involvement of a consultant depends on the answer to these questions: how long has the institution been involved in planning? How well received is planning on campus?

The duration of a planning process often determines the need for an outside planning consultant. Often a consultant is needed to help get a planning process going and usually facilitates a fledgling planning process. Also, a long-standing planning process may require the assistance of a consultant if the direction or style of the process is undergoing dramatic change and a change agent is considered beneficial. More often than not, a consultant is helpful to a process in its beginning stages, as a channel for credibility and comparison to other processes. It is a rarer event when an institution requires a consultant's help in delivering the message that the process is following a different path or delivering some difficult news. A prophet is never heard in his or her own land.

Who Drives the Planning Process? Typically, the president drives the planning efforts at most colleges and universities. His or her impetus may have been derived from discussions with trustees (and they need to be fully supportive or the entire exercise is in vain) or just from a personal belief in the importance of planning. Nonetheless, if anyone other than the president leads this process, the process inevitably will fail. Success begins at the top.

Who Typically Manages the Planning Process? Managing the planning process generally is coordinated by the institutional planning officer. In the absence of a formal planning office, the finance officer often will take charge. After that, the exceptions are as numerous as there are colleges in the United States. Whoever manages the planning process ultimately works closely with four key people (and this scenario *rarely* varies): the president, the provost, the finance officer, and the human resource director.

What Else Is Happening on Campus?

It is important to link the planning process with other key institutional processes, such as operational budgeting, enrollment projections, introduction of new academic programs, and fundraising campaigns, just to name a few. Obviously, a good planning process works hand in hand to initiate many of those efforts, but often planning occurs while many of these activities are already underway.

It is important to begin planning so that budget preparations for the next fiscal cycle(s) can be coordinated with established goals and objectives. It is essential to time the process so that communication with key groups does not occur during vacation or examination periods. Link planning cycles with planned fundraising campaigns, enrollment increases or decreases, staffing adjustments, or major capital investments. These may sound like elementary premises, but many institutions find themselves trying to use their planning process to justify many ill-timed activities, rather than allowing the process to guide an institutional response to new opportunities and challenges.

Communication Is Critical

Many different types of communication should be employed at the beginning of a planning process and should be diligently continued as the process proceeds. Just as there are many different groups involved in the planning process, so there are many different ways to communicate. Every method, from group meetings or forums, to written memorandums and updates, to subcommittee and task force meetings should be employed.

One helpful device for establishing a communication plan includes identifying the various audiences and understanding how best to communicate the planning process with them. For example, it might be most effective to meet with trustees in a small group session (often best with the help of a consultant), while possibly introducing a letter campaign to alumni from the president. Often task forces and subcommittees are a good way to expand group participation and keep everyone informed. A regular series of update memorandums to faculty and staff supplements occasional group meetings where questions and comments are viable. No matter which combination of devices are selected for the communications plan, make sure to have matched the plan to the personality of the campus community. Some audiences like to hear, some audiences like to see, and some audiences just like to read in the privacy of their offices what is occurring. Provide options and ample opportunities!

Many schools have conducted a wonderful, all-involving planning process and then wasted much time and paper producing a weighty, wordy report.

The role of the human resource department in helping with the communications plan is an important one. No department knows better the collective personality of that particular college or university. Without the input from the human resource staff, a communications plan may suffer credibility or clarity. Since an effective communications effort ensures the long-standing success of institutional planning, it remains in the institution's best interest to seek assistance from the office that deals directly with communications on campus.

Continuous Implementation

The biggest mistake college and university planning groups make is to wait until the process is almost complete to begin implementation of planning goals and objectives. Many institutions have conducted a wonderful, all-involving planning process and then wasted much time and paper producing a weighty, wordy report. Nothing reduces the credibility of a planning process more than waiting too long for implementation, further compounded by an over-circulated and underread planning report.

Implementation is essential and should be ongoing from the moment the process begins. Continuous implementation is a critical activity to ensure that the process is as vital as circulating the final written report. People get discouraged when the process drags on without tangible evidence of activity.

Pitfalls and Challenges

The planning process has begun. The institutional history has been revisited, the campus climate has been assessed, the importance of community building has been asserted, the right groups of people have been involved. Everyone has heard the planning message repeatedly and clearly. Institutional goals have been identified and verified, staffing needs for the next three decades have been mapped out, and the operating plan is implemented in a meaningful way. What are the next steps?

Two bits of advice may prove helpful as the planning process goes forward. First, stay flexible and adaptable. Remember that *planning* and *life* often occur simultaneously. Planning does not always drive institutional activity; in fact, it rarely does. Instead, opportunities usually arise and a good planning process ensures that an institution is ready to respond appropriately.

Second, remember that different groups view a planning process differently at different times. This scenario is one of the hardest to overcome. Many times a planning process has started with the endorsement and support of one group, only to find that halfway into the process that same group began to speak out against that very same process. Be assured this behavior is normal for the members of any academic institution. The blessing and the curse of an academic culture is that it remains a changeable, unpredictable environment (not unlike some other cultures, but worse than many). A solid understanding and appreciation of organizational behavior helps immensely and can maintain sanity.

Notes

1. Cohen, M. D. and J. G. March. 1974. *Leadership and Ambiguity.* New York: McGraw Hill, p. 325, 329.
2. Cohen and March, *Leadership and Ambiguity*, p. 47.
3. Cohen and March, *Leadership and Ambiguity*, p. 48.
4. Baldridge, V. and G. L. Riley. 1977. *Governing Academic Organization.* Berkeley: McCutchan Publishing.
5. March, J. G. 1982. "Emerging Developments in the Study of Organizations." *The Review of Higher Education*, 6 (1), p. 1-17.
6. March, "Emerging Developments," p. 1.

4

What about Budgeting?

James H. Manifold

The institutional budget is the mechanism through which most elements of the strategic plan are realized. The budget is a financial plan used to estimate and control the operations of an organization.

If an institution initiates a new academic program, it will be reflected in the budget. If there is a new emphasis on fringe benefits, it will be in the budget. If a department or program is being eliminated, that too will be reflected in the budget.

There are many reasons to prepare an annual budget. Some institutions are obliged to do so by state law. Others see this requirement in the bylaws of the institution. The budget process may be the only time when all elements of the institution are seen as one enterprise. Communication and coordination are essential. During this process, most employees in responsible positions are asked to participate in the planning process. The finished budget can be used to control operations during the year and serve as a framework for measuring performance at year end.

If there are such good reasons to budget, why then is budgeting such an unpopular activity at most institutions? The reasons are as varied as the number of people who feel forced to participate in this annual exercise. Because the vocabulary of budgeting is based in accounting, and many deans, vice presidents, and department heads are not schooled in this discipline, budgeting seems arcane and alien to some. Others, perhaps more clever than confused, prefer not to be committed to the performance requirements implicit in signing off on a budget. And everyone can find more pressing problems to devote limited time, rather than sit down and plan for the coming year. This last reason may be the most comfortable yet the weakest of all. For those entrusted with the present and future life of an institution, planning is the single most important activity. It is the essence of management. The most important thing to realize about the budgeting process is that the budget itself is not the final product. It is evidence that the planning activity has, in fact, taken place.

By charter and logic, the trustees are ultimately responsible for establishing the requirement that a budget is prepared and seeing to it that it is done. But trustees cannot accomplish this important task alone. That falls to those "on the ground": faculty, administrators, and in some cases, students.

As in almost any significant human enterprise, leadership is critical to success. The leader will vary depending on the size and nature of the institution as well as the personalities involved. The driving force in planning could be the chair of the board, the chair of the budget and finance committee, the president, the chief financial officer, the provost, or the vice president for planning.

In the broadest sense, the most important point is that someone in the organization takes responsibility for the process and motivates the participants.

Process

Because the fiscal well-being of an institution is the responsibility of the board of trustees, annual budgets are presented to and approved by this body. The nature of the process that leads up to this moment is a function of the culture of the institution. In its simplest form, the president and chief financial officer might sit down at the end of the year, review the results of operations and put together a simple budget for the coming year. It might be based on the financial position of the school and provide for tuition and salary increases. A more elaborate, consensus management approach is described later. Many institutions' processes fall somewhere between these extremes.

Due to the extensive responsibilities of trustees, their diverse individual talents, and their limited time to commit to the college, the work of a board often is divided into specialized committees, e.g., academic policy, student affairs, fundraising, and finance or budget committees.

Since budgeting often is viewed as a seasonal process, the budget committee may only meet during a certain part of the year. If the fiscal year aligns with the academic year, the budget committee usually will convene in September or October after the annual audited financial statements are available. It will meet periodically to set budget guidelines, review financial models, set priorities based on the strategic plan, and finally, in the spring, approve a budget to be taken to the full board of trustees for approval before the new fiscal year begins.

The membership of the committee is composed of trustees, who are responsible members, administrators based on their functional roles at the college, constituent members of the faculty, and increasingly, student members.

Trustee members are chosen based on their particular background and interest. The administrators will vary by institution, but usually will include the chief executive officer, the chief academic officer, and the chief financial officer. Faculty and students may be appointed, elected, or serve by virtue of the office they hold, e.g., chairperson of the faculty senate or treasurer of the student council.

One of the keys to ensure constituent members are effective is to develop a mechanism to allow them to report back to their constituencies. Otherwise these individuals often will wind up representing themselves.

Due to the policy nature of the trustee budget committee and the time limitations placed on this group, the chief executive officer often will develop an "on-campus" committee that consists of the nontrustee membership to work on the details of the budget and ensure consensus before it gets to the trustee level.

The most successful budgets involve many other individuals in the institution, sometimes even the account supervisors

One of the keys to ensure constituent members are effective is to develop a mechanism to allow them to report back to their constituencies.

and other frontline personnel. This is where the knowledge about current costs resides (who but the librarians can know that the cost of periodicals is increasing 17 percent?) and where the implementation of the final budget will be made.

Those who have participated in a budgeting exercise are keenly aware that it is every bit a political as well as a financial exercise. It is the process of allocating scarce resources to a plethora of worthy projects. If the institution has done a good job of long-range planning, the difficult choices will be resolved by measuring the decisions against congruency with the long-range plan.

Types of Budgets

The first critical distinction in budgeting is to separate capital budgets from operating budgets. Capital budgets concern the acquisition or rehabilitation of assets with a life of more than one year, such as buildings, equipment, and landscape projects. The institution needs to decide at the outset what commitments it desires to make in this area. Commingling capital and operating budgets together pits people against buildings. In this contest people always win and the consequence is deferred maintenance, a problem that has become a national disease in higher education.

The Operating Budget

A good place to start the budgeting exercise is with a forecast of revenues. With the exception of the most well-endowed research institutions, the single largest revenue source is student charges for tuition, room, and board. While some institutions prefer to connect tuition revenue with education and general expense and room and board revenue with their associated expenditures called auxiliary enterprises, this split is a largely artificial accounting distinction from a budgetary perspective. Even without the arbitrary element of cost allocating, the revenue generating possibilities of these three sources ought to be determined by market conditions, as well as cost, with the goal of providing revenues for the operations of the institution.

For research institutions, the next largest revenue source may be government grants. Most of these revenues are tied directly to research expenditures. The discretionary portion is called "indirect cost recovery" which means a contribution to overhead for the institution. This revenue source from administrative overhead was capped in 1993 by the federal government at 26 percent of direct costs.

Income from endowments can be a significant revenue source. For institutions with small endowments, this item is budgeted as the estimated dividend and interest income the investments in stocks and bonds will provide. For well endowed institutions, the issue is more complicated.

A seminal study sponsored by the Ford Foundation in 1968 revealed that colleges and universities were experiencing poor returns on their endowment investments because of an overweighing in bonds over stocks in the portfolio. The cause of this bias was that spendable income was being defined according to the trust law concept of income that segregated interest and dividends (income) from realized gains (principal). The study recommended that colleges and universities invest for the long term and that the spendable income from endowment be defined as a percentage of average market value. This rethinking of endowment income was an enormously liberating doctrine that gave institutions permission to invest for long-term growth, secure in the knowledge that their "income" would be available for spending regardless of how it was earned, as interest from bonds, dividends from stock, realized gains from real estate investments, or even unrealized gains from portfolio appreciation.

The most useful gifts to an institution are made with no strings attached. These are called unrestricted gifts.

For these colleges, the investment decisions revolve around asset allocation weighting and budget decisions around the appropriate percentage of market value for the spending rate. Generally, 5 percent is considered a prudent long-term spending rate.

Gifts can be a significant source of operating revenues. The most useful gifts to an institution are made with no strings attached. These are called unrestricted gifts. The next most useful gifts are restricted gifts where the restriction is to an expenditure the institution would make in any case, e.g., faculty salaries, building maintenance, or scholarships. These kinds of restricted gifts are often called program-supporting or budget-relieving gifts. The least useful gift, from a budgetary point of view, is a restricted gift that provokes new spending outside the budget. Examples of these kinds of gifts include: a specific faculty member's travel to an international conference (that was not budgeted and would not be funded before other budgeted faculty travel), a staff retreat to an expensive resort, or a collection of rare books in a field of study not taught at the college. The last general category of revenues is often called other sources or miscellaneous income. This category might include rental of facilities to outside organizations, summer conference income, etc.

On the expense side, there are a variety of methods of sorting the expenditures. The two most common are: expenditures by cost center and expenditures by nature. Cost centers refer to the traditional financial statement presentation outlined in the 1973 *Audit Guide for Colleges and Universities* prepared by the American Institute of Certified Public Accountants (AICPA). It is fast becoming out of date due to the recent pronouncements issued for nonprofit entities by the Financial Accounting Standards Board (FASB).

In addition, a new comprehensive audit guide for all nonprofit organizations was released in April of 1995 in exposure draft format. The new guide aligns with the FASB pronouncements in providing considerable latitude in reporting format. Over time, college and university financial statement presentation may well mirror corporate financial statements in style and content.

A jurisdictional battle waged in 1991 between FASB and the Governmental Accounting Standards Board (GASB) finds higher education in the altogether unsatisfying position of having one segment—private colleges and universities—following the new FASB reporting standards, while public colleges and universities follow GASB, with the AICPA *Audit Guide* trying to bridge the two.

Since the old audit guide is the public school standard and continues in effect for private schools as the format for their historical data, it is a good place to start.

The audit guide sees two major cost centers, "education and general expenditures" and "auxiliary enterprises." As discussed earlier, auxiliary enterprises are composed of the room and board activities of the college. This cost center also may include the bookstore (if run by the institution) and other business activities such as parking lots.

The education and general expenditures cost center contains the remaining spending activities and are subdivided into the following cost centers: instruction, academic support, student services, institutional support, public service, research, operations and maintenance of plant, and scholarships and fellowships. Both major cost centers also may have what are called mandatory transfers. These are the principal and interest payments to amortize long-term debt.

Appearing below all of these expenditures is a section called voluntary transfers that record interfund transfers either out of or into the operating fund. Such transfers out may include a large unrestricted bequest that the board of trustees wishes to go into a quasiendowment. Transfers in might be from quasiendowment to mask an operating deficit.

Although the cost center approach to organizing expenditures conforms to the traditional financial presentation, most budget committees prefer to see expenditures by nature. This sorting would start with salaries and wages and their associated fringe benefits. Other expenditures might include staff development expenditures, travel and entertainment, utilities, office supplies, insurance, etc. All of these categories in turn can be subdivided, e.g., salaries and wages can be broken out as faculty salaries, staff support salaries, and student wages. Utilities can be subdivided to electric, gas, water, telephone, etc., and even further by building.

Sorting expenditures by nature allows those involved with the budget process to isolate these costs and use financial models that can increase or decrease like expenditures by differing percentages. If health insurance costs are rising faster than office supplies or utilities, these can be factored into the model. Under a cost center model, a labor intensive cost center (such as instruction) could be disadvantaged if all cost center budget increases were to be held to the same percentage increase.

Spreadsheet Software

The advent of personal computers and inexpensive spreadsheet software has allowed all institutions to develop financial budget models. Lotus 1-2-3™ and Excel™ software are representative of this genre.

Spreadsheets allow the user to construct operating statements of revenues and expenditures. These models often will show the last year's actual numbers and the current year's budget numbers. In the spaces for the next year's budget, instead of numbers, the model builder can put in a formula. This formula is invisible to the reader of the budget model. The formula can use numbers in the spreadsheet for the current budget combined with certain other variables elsewhere in the spreadsheet and generate a number. For example, for student tuition the formula may be to go to one assumption of how many students are estimated for next year and multiply it by the tuition rate for that year. The gift income figure may be built by going to the current year's budget number and increasing it by some percentage found elsewhere in the spreadsheet.

While the foregoing is a simplified discussion of this topic, it should be noted that the budget model can get exceedingly complicated. Often one model will contain a series of submodels that calculate financial aid or investment income using a variety of assumptions before producing one lonely line item in the budget. With each year, the model may be improved with some new algorithm or additional submodel.

There are many advantages of financial budget models. Almost any institution can create for itself a custom tool to forecast the next budget year or indeed the next 10 years. A variety of "what if" scenarios can be played out in seconds where before it might have taken a week to construct just one on paper. In the early stages of budgeting, such scenarios inform the budget committee about the parameters of the possible and allow for some early goal setting.

As with most good things in life, there are some traps. In the case of spreadsheets, care must be made to ensure the model is working as planned. Each line should be documented so the numbers being produced are accurate. A change in one formula may have an unintended effect on another area of the model. A good discipline is to have an individual "prove" the numbers in the model independently at the start of each budget season to make sure nothing has crept into the model that would produce a false number. Most spreadsheets allow for the addition of text to be added to the various lines that describe the calculations. This text can be in the spreadsheet but outside the boundaries that will be printed. This trail can be helpful to those who maintain the model after it has been established.

Cost Behavior

A discussion of budgeting would not be complete without some reference to cost behavior. For higher education, a critical distinction can be made between fixed and variable costs. Fixed costs tend to be constant regardless of the level of educational activity at the institution. Examples include certain administrative costs, such as the president's salary, property insurance, and electricity to light the campus at night. Variable costs are sensitive to the level of activity and increase or decrease accordingly. Examples include utility consumption in dormitories, office supplies for academic departments, and salary expense for adjunct faculty hired to teach additional sections. A careful look at the costs of most colleges and universities reveals that 75 to 90 percent of all expenditures exhibit fixed-cost behavior. Tenured faculty, buildings and grounds maintenance, and administrative staffing cannot easily be increased and decreased depending on the level of student registrations. This condition presents real challenges to those involved with the budgeting process.

Changing direction is less like driving a sports car and more like steering an oil tanker at sea. In higher education institutions, the need for strategic planning is of paramount importance.

Special Role of Human Resource Professionals

Historically, education has been a labor-intensive process. Unlike many other activities in the twentieth century that have been able to use technology as a substitute for human labor, in higher education, technology is more often seen as a way of enhancing or improving the educational product.

In most colleges and universities, salaries and wages (and their associated fringe benefits) comprise the single largest expense category, ranging from one-third to one-half of all expenditures. It is therefore essential that human resource professionals be involved centrally in the budget process. The nature of this involvement will depend on the institution. The human resource department will need to be apprised of the budgeted faculty and staff positions including rank or pay

Changing direction is less like driving a sports car and more like steering an oil tanker at sea. In higher education institutions, the need for strategic planning is of paramount importance.

grade, contemplated salary and wage increases, and any benefits changes. The final item may be initiated by the institution or be the effect of changes in state or federal law. Accurate forecasts of salaries, turnover, and fringe benefits can make or break a budget. In today's personnel environment, legal and tax issues are becoming increasingly complex and costly.

In addition, a proactive human resource department can reduce costs for its institution in a number of areas. The maintenance of an equitable wage and salary program will improve morale, reduce turnover (and the costs of recruiting), and increase productivity. The creation of a safe working environment avoids unnecessary workers' compensation and disability claims. Such efforts will be rewarded by lower insurance premiums and legal expenditures.

Those involved with the budgeting process realize early on that the sooner the human resource professionals are involved in budgeting decisions, the better. Many hours can be wasted pursuing a planning initiative with a component that violates state labor laws, federal tax codes, or antidiscrimination legislation. A human resource professional would be aware of these limitations and could suggest acceptable alternatives that accomplish the same goals.

Relationship to the Strategic Plan

The budget is the mechanism through which most elements of the strategic plan are realized. This is because most strategic initiatives require resources and the budgeting process is the vehicle for allocating resources.

The link between the strategic plan and the budgeting process is not automatic and should not be taken for granted. Especially in a consensus management environment, high turnover in constituent membership means that, for many, planning begins with their arrival date.

To guard against this dynamic, the senior members of the planning process will need to develop a methodology to educate new members about the institutional priorities of the strategic plan and a discipline to ensure the final budget reflects these priorities by rewarding them with additional resources. For example, if an engineering school has established a planning priority to broaden the liberal arts education of its students, then there should be new faculty positions in the humanities and fine arts, not in physics. If the strategic plan sets a goal of improving staff morale, a new child care center might be found in the budget, not a salary freeze.

As logical as this sounds, nothing should be taken for granted. It is better to build into each step of the budgeting process formal reviews (or reality checks) that specifically reflect on how, at this point in the budgeting process, the goals of the strategic plan are being addressed.

It is only through this deliberate effort that the budgeting process can be an instrument to accomplish the strategic plan. Absent this effort, the strategic plan always will be a plan about the future, frozen in the past.

5

Rightsizing

Kathleen M. Alvino

Human Resource Management Role in Strategic Personnel Planning

The human resource department is an integral partner in strategic planning. Within its areas of responsibility, the department assists an institution in facilitating and managing all aspects of personnel needs, such as employment, training, compensation, benefits, and labor relations including all associated costs. The human resource department is responsible for conducting an ongoing dialogue of diminishing and increasing personnel needs with its customers. Today higher education is faced with changing economic conditions and a changing work force. Now, more than at any other time, the human resource professional needs to be involved intrically in an institution's development of a strategic personnel plan that will enhance the ability to meet the flow of changing needs and conditions that face higher education.

In this chapter we are going to focus on personnel staffing within the strategic planning process by posing and answering some questions. How does a college or university's human resource department develop a plan for providing the institution with a flexible, quality work force, yet strengthen control of personnel costs? What is the definition of "rightsizing" and how can an institution go about the process of rightsizing? How is rightsizing used in the planning process as an ongoing tool to manage staffing? Is the institution unionized, and if so, how does the institution work with unions in relation to the rightsizing process? How does the human resource professional carefully plan for participation in the overall strategic planning process? How does the human resource department go about developing an outline for implementation and communication of the strategic plan? What is the measurement of a plan's success or failure?

Rightsizing is determining a personnel plan to place the right people in the right positions at a fair salary. An overall personnel planning concept, defined as rightsizing, is an adaptive response by human resource professionals to a dynamic institutional planning process.

Awareness of the politics of the process, the effect on the organization, and the options for helping employees understand and support its presence need to be considered.

Arriving at the "right size" organization composed of a flexible, quality staff, may begin with some initial personnel reduction or reallocation. Strategies need to be incorporated in the plan to enable human resource professionals to deal with these possible occurrences.

Strategic Planning Process

To facilitate an understanding of human resource management's inherent value to an institution and its role in strategic planning, it is essential for the human resource professional to work continuously to promote the services the department provides, to be seen as the barometer of the morale of the staff and faculty, to be apolitical and provide the objective, fair viewpoint (not always politically popular or safe, but necessary), and to hold the reputation for trust, nonpartiality, and confidentiality. The human resource department needs to be an essential part of the financial discussion in strategic planning and should be diligent in working closely with finance to monitor the costs of salaries and benefits. The human resource department needs to work continuously to assist the institution in controlling personnel expenses that typically can comprise 55 to 65 percent of a college or university's operational budget.

The strategic planning process should be a living, breathing plan as outlined in previous chapters. It is never finished; it is a rolling process in which people can make adjustments along the way to new challenges. The human resource department can use strategic human resource planning tools such as job performance evaluation, training, succession planning, interdepartmental assignments, temporary assignments, part-time assignments, lateral transfers, and flexibility of the staff to assist an institution in meeting its overall strategic goals.

The human resource department's strategic planning priorities focus on several areas:

Rightsizing is determining a plan to place the right people in the right positions at the right rate of compensation.

— managing the financial effect on the institution by controlling human resource costs in the form of salaries and benefits;

— planning strategically for replacing personnel as positions become open due to promotions, resignations, or retirements and providing advancement opportunities through succession planning;

— providing ongoing training of personnel to help increase productivity and provide job enrichment; and

— providing ways in which people can grow for their own benefit, as well as for the benefit of the college or university. There are hidden savings when an institution is able to extract quality work from quality people who are properly oriented, trained, and strongly committed to the institution.

Rightsizing-Downsizing

As noted previously, rightsizing is determining a plan to place the right people in the right positions at the right rate of compensation. The continuous goal of the human resource strategic planning process is to place the most qualified individual into a position that will use his or her talents to the fullest, yet allow room for flexibility if circumstances warrant. Rightsizing has fluidity in that it has the ability to increase or decrease personnel numbers or can be used to reorganize jobs to fit the needs of the institution at any given point in time. It is a planning tool that is essential to support the mission and goals of an institution.

Downsizing is the reduction of staffing levels to meet changing economic, demographic, or financial conditions. Downsizing can be reactionary. Downsizing is visual in that the institution as a whole can see and feel the effects of the changing conditions in which the institution operates. Although downsizing may be necessary, it is not a method of choice.

Downsizing can be a knee-jerk reaction to the need to cut costs. People become the most visible target, the easy solution that gives the appearance of the administration taking decisive action. Downsizing, in fact, can be the worst road to take. With downsizing comes reduced morale, uncertainty, mourning for those who have left, and fear that it could happen again. The result is not only personnel reduction, but also reduced productivity.

If an institution is challenged continuously with further downsizing, the original analysis of institutional needs may not have been done honestly because the depth of projected adverse economic conditions was either not believed or avoided. The president might not be able to face up to the reality or the reality was not politically acceptable. Many CEOs lack the courage to carry out what financial projections dictate. They hope a small reduction of personnel and expenses will take care of the problem and everything will return to normal. Some presidents are lucky with this type of action; most are not.

In all too many cases the human resource department is not consulted or is not part of any reduction planning process. Rather, the human resource department is used as the executionist. The president, the finance vice president, and a few selected others discuss the changing economic circumstances, make a decision to reduce personnel, and instruct the human resource professionals to carry out the staff reductions. If the human resource department protests the decision, the department is seen as an obstacle, not a team player. When the human resource department carries out the downsizing, the department is perceived by the faculty and staff as powerless—a tool of the administration and not the advocate for the people. Credibility is lost.

If downsizing is chosen as the course of action, the institution should do everything possible to make it a onetime occurrence. In other words, if it becomes necessary to downsize, make all the needed cuts so the surgery remains a onetime operation. The CUPA publication *You Can Get There From Here: The Road to Downsizing in Higher Education*, by Barbara Butterfield with Susan Wolfe, is an excellent resource.[1]

The Rightsizing Process

Rather than downsizing, a better path would be to strategically plan for human resource staffing changes so that adjustments can be made easily and completed quickly when they occur. With the goal of rightsizing and appropriate and well thought out human resource planning in place, the institution should be able to weather changing conditions that affect the day-to-day environment without reverting continuously to a downsizing situation.

Where to Begin?

The first major question that needs to be answered is: "What is the future vision for the institution?" The president, in consultation with the board of trustees, needs to establish and communicate the vision the college or university will focus on for the short term and the long term. This vision becomes the basis for the institution's strategic planning process that includes the human resource department.

As an example, if the president's vision is that the institution will be the international leader in a particular field of education—the best art and design school in the world with an international reputation for excellence in quality of faculty, staff, facilities, and student life—the planning goals that might be established in support of that vision are:

— develop a plan to be on the leading edge of new technology in the specific fields of art and design;

— utilize the strengths of a diverse internal community to gain commitment to the vision;

— establish a campus planning process to provide top-notch facilities;

— enhance development efforts to support the financial needs of the vision;

— determine staffing needs to meet the current and future goals of the institution's vision.

From these broad goals, the various parts of the institution will begin to develop the planning strategy to support the overall future vision.

The administration should act prudently to prepare the budget in concert with the strategic planning goals in three scenarios—best case, status quo, and worst case formats based on admissions, development, and financial projections. By doing so, the organization will be prepared for all contingencies. If strategic planning works well and if the college or university finds itself in a precarious financial situation due to reduced state support, or loss or reduction in grants and gifts, or a victim of changing demographics and student choices, the administration will be prepared to deal with the circumstances in a well thought out approach.

As part of personnel planning in three scenarios, the human resource department also should plan three scenarios and begin the process by analyzing faculty and staff needs and the associated expenses. Human resource professionals should perform an analysis of the skills of the institution's current personnel, assess the training needs, and develop a plan to address the type of training that should be provided. If not being done currently as part of the normal human resource department operation, the human resource professionals should begin a process of benchmarking with other like institutions to compare and contrast the way similar needs are being met.

Once needs are determined, the human resource department should work in conjunction with academic affairs, finance, and development, as well as other appropriate areas of the college, to formulate a general plan that is flexible and fluid. This process will look at the short-term and long-term personnel needs and related costs, always keeping in mind the strategic goals that are to be met.

The administration should act prudently to prepare the budget in concert with the strategic planning goals in three scenarios— best case, status quo, and worst case formats based on admissions, development, and financial projections.

The Right Size

When determining the "right" size and composition of an institution's work force, there are several key objectives that should be considered and continuously planned for in advance:

— motivate strong performers to continue to be energized by new and continuing challenges;

— motivate lesser performers to take on responsibilities that might better fit their individual talents;

— provide upward progression, as well as lateral movement that can broaden an individual's knowledge and make them more valuable and flexible;

— avoid the shortsightedness of redefining or eliminating a job that displaces a talented individual;

— look at areas of the college where a talented but displaced person could fit and then plan to outplace the poorer performer.

How to Facilitate the
Human Resource Planning Process

Remember that human resource planning touches every part of a college or university. The institution's senior strategic planning group must realize that development of a personnel staffing plan needs to be done carefully and thoroughly to ensure success.

For a broad spectrum of the community to understand and accept a plan, the process of strategic human resource planning needs to be done carefully and collaboratively. Guidelines that can be used in strategic human resource planning are: (1) establish a planning group; (2) develop a forecast; (3) cost the plan; (4) communicate the plan; (5) obtain labor agreement; (6) obtain a legal review; and (7) implement the plan.

Phase I—Establish a Planning Group

Since human resource management is considered a staff function, the department usually does not have a well-established power base to implement change on its own. It is essential to establish a planning group that will work with the human resource department to analyze the current work force and also review and determine any proposed adjustments, additions, or eliminations of positions. The human resource department cannot perform this task in a vacuum. The human resource professional must be aware of the politics of this process. It is essential to work with the planning group to facilitate group trust and to help the group members understand that they need to remain as objective as possible.

When choosing members of the planning group, attempt to include well-respected individuals from all institutional levels who are connected to the formal, as well as the informal, organization. A "nonstakeholder," should be designated as the point person to facilitate disputes among the group's members objectively. At a mature institution, this nonstakeholder may be the chief human resource officer. It is key that the human resource professional always be viewed as apolitical, fair, nonjudgmental, and act as the "resident conscience" to the president and senior staff.

Once the group is set, data collection needs to begin. There are several methods to carry out this process. It might be preferable to have the human resource representative, or a small subcommittee of the larger group, meet individually with area deans, vice presidents, and directors to get a sketch of needs, objectives, and financial concerns and then bring that data back to the larger human resource planning group for dissection and digestion. If the organization is the type that openly shares information, the deans, vice presidents, and directors might be invited to speak to the entire group regarding staffing needs. Whatever provides the best sense of trust and confidence by the various campus constituencies within a particular college or university is the method that should be followed.

Phase II—Develop a Forecast

Once the data have been collected, a methodical layout through organizational chart form or other visual tool should be developed to see how the suggested organization looks. Graphic presentation usually yields a clearer picture of where the organization is and where the organization thinks it wants to go.

From this point, the planning group should compare the old with the new organizational structure and identify a list of additions, deletions, and possible transfers. The group should then begin to lay out steps to facilitate needed adjustments or changes. The changes could include reassigning of individuals; hiring more people in some areas and reducing personnel in other areas; identifying a need to hire more part-time people, or have employees job share; establishing a plan to hire people to perform seasonal work during peak times of the academic year; or possibly contracting out some job functions altogether.

A careful analysis of the background and quality of the current work force needs to be completed to identify a pool of talent that could be used across area functions or that could be used better in other positions.

In doing strategic personnel planning, the human resource department is always faced with turnover from resignation, retirement, etc. It is at these points in time that an effective human resource plan becomes invaluable because departing personnel can be replaced easily and smoothly if potential replacements already have been identified and trained for a future job. A strategic personnel plan also would contain contingencies to move a particular position's funds to another identified area where a position may be needed. If through the previous analysis of position requirements there are extra moneys identified as becoming available during the plan year, the strategic planning group should consider what human resource enhancements or needs should be given first priority through use of the extra funds.

If the decision is reached to replace a departing employee while maintaining the position, the human resource planning model will have identified potential replacements or determined that the position will need to be filled with outside personnel. The identification of individuals, the analysis of qualifications and potential, the discussion of individuals who are promotable or who can move into more expanded responsibilities is part of a process known as succession planning.

Succession planning is a well used tool in the private sector. It is often talked about in higher education and sometimes even used, but not often. Succession planning at the upper levels of higher education administration is rarely a reality due to the specialization of individuals. A search process usually is conducted since it is such an ingrained part of the culture of higher education. Although an interim replacement might be

A careful analysis of the background and quality of the current work force needs to be completed to identify a pool of talent that could be used across area functions or that could be used better in other positions.

designated, it is the unusual case that a cross-institutional successor simply would be appointed. The problem of individual specialization can be overcome if talented individuals with strong potential are identified and provided with training for other identified positions over time.

At the lower levels, it is possible to use succession planning effectively in higher education since skills are more easily transferable or enhanced through training.

As a caution, if there is a situation where a quality person is going to be displaced, the human resource planning group should assess where this person could be relocated and a lesser talented individual removed. These types of contemplations and discussions can be completed by the group in conjunction with the appropriate area vice president.

If the worst-case scenario occurs and cost reduction is required, the institution should first consider addressing areas of general college operating expenses that can be reduced other than personnel costs. These considerations might be the containment of all but necessary travel expenses to support developmental efforts, or a freeze on purchases, etc.

If the previous operational cutbacks do not satisfy correction of the financial deficit, the human resource planning process initially should consider a hiring freeze, merit increase curtailment, or a pay reduction across the board. If these efforts fail to address the budget difficulties, direct personnel reductions might become a consideration.

Phase III—Cost the Plan

Once the determination has been made on the size, composition, and distribution of the work force, the planning group needs to cost out the changes and determine what, if any, delta exists. If done properly, i.e., with honesty and without much political influence, the human resource planning group will be able to develop a plan for a more productive work force composed of fewer full-time positions with more flexibility in terms of transferable skills. The main objective is to attempt to keep the human resource personnel related expenses at a proportional or reduced percentage to the overall institutional budget.

If savings have been identified through the strategic planning process, the human resource strategic planning group should prepare a proposal for the use or nonuse of any identified excess funds. Reserving part of any identified savings in case the planning process meets with unforeseen snags or problems is always a wise choice.

Phase IV—Communicate the Plan

While the strategic human resource planning group works on its analysis and plan, a simultaneous awareness of the effect of the group's deliberations on the culture and politics of the campus community needs to be recognized and addressed.

Continuous communications in the form of updates and progress reports should be distributed to the president, deans, vice presidents, faculty, staff, and students. A planning process, if it is to live long and prosper, cannot be a secretive process. The process must be open to the campus community so there are no suspected hidden agendas or unexpected results. For a planning process to be successful, the campus community must feel that it has had an opportunity to participate and to be heard in the debate. If communication is not part of the institution's planning process, the process is doomed to failure. There is no need to go into a lengthy discussion of the importance of communication and participation in higher education. *Use it or die a slow, painful death.*

Phase V—Obtain Labor Agreement

If the college or university has labor unions and proposed human resource changes might affect unionized personnel, the human resource professional must work with the union or unions through the bargaining process to obtain agreement to proposed changes. The institution might have the individual responsible for labor relations as part of the human resource planning group from the beginning. Early union involvement is essential so that timely, effective dialogues can be held.

In general, if union personnel are not affected adversely and the terms and conditions of the contract are not violated, this phase of human resource planning should be fairly straightforward and simply provide an opportunity for discussion.

If violations do take place or changes to the contract are required, be prepared for lengthy, tedious negotiations.

Approaching union matters with the contract's terms and conditions in mind is always prudent to avoid a most unpleasant derailing of the planning process for an undetermined length of time. With labor unions, doing the homework and being upfront is advised strongly. This action saves time and assists in building relationships and trust that can be used in future negotiations.

Phase VI—Obtain a Legal Review

The legal counsel's review process analyzes the proposed changes against the possible promotion or demotion of individuals, as well as possible transfers of individuals or reduction in hours in view of age, gender, and ethnic background.

Once the plan has been formulated, a review of the proposed changes by legal counsel is advisable. The legal counsel can look at the proposed aggregate changes in terms of possible discrimination violations. The legal counsel's review process analyzes the proposed changes against the possible promotion or demotion of individuals, as well as possible transfers of individuals or reduction in hours in view of age, gender, and ethnic background. If an institution has in-house legal expertise in discrimination matters, this review can be accomplished internally, but sometimes a completely objective view of the personnel planning proposal can provide a better warning system and safeguard against possible future charges.

Phase VII—Implement the Plan

Once the plan is developed and has been reviewed and approved by the president, the senior administrative group, and legal counsel, the process and its outcome should be communicated to the campus community so they feel a part of the process, "buy-in" to the three-plan scenario and the resulting planned changes, and view the process as fair and open.

If there are individuals whose job status will change, the responsible human resource professional should contact the area dean or supervisor and provide advice on how to approach the individual employee and communicate the forthcoming status changes. The first-line supervisor must take ownership and responsibility for the changes and become part of the planning process. Human resource department personnel can act as the coordinators or advisers to the supervisor, but should not be the communicator. The human resource department's responsibility is to facilitate the process objectively and act as the internal consultant, not take on the supervisor's role.

In summary, once the initial plan has been designed and approved and successfully implemented, the human resource department, in conjunction with the strategic planning group, has the responsibility to review the progress and success or failure of the various phases of the plan. The human resource department needs to report the findings of the review to the president and senior staff on an ongoing basis. Periodic communication with the general community also would be wise to keep faculty and staff informed of the status of the strategic planning process in its various phases.

The strategic human resource planning group should continue its role and meet as required to fine tune the plan or change it if conditions dictate.

If an institution recognizes the wisdom of personnel planning and the concept of rightsizing and its importance to the future of an organization, a college or university will be able to meet the challenges that lie ahead.

Notes

1. Butterfield, Barbara with Susan Wolfe. 1994. *You Can Get There from Here: The Road to Downsizing in Higher Education.* Washington, DC: College and University Personnel Association.

6

Faculty and Staff Benefits: Meeting the Challenge of Difficult Financial Times

Robert M. Wilson

The Golden Age of Benefits

For a generation or more, until the late 1980s, colleges and universities responded generously and often eagerly to faculty and staff needs for enhanced benefits. Benefits programs—seen to be relatively low in cost and essential to attract and retain the best people—grew steadily but haphazardly over time.

In this period of growth both the value and cost of benefits increased dramatically, driven by many factors. These factors included institutional philosophies that responded to changing times; competitive pressures from peer institutions; internal "lobbies" and collective bargaining agreements; the desire

This golden age of benefits program enhancement ended in the late 1980s as the dark clouds of financial concern turned into full-blown firestorms in budget crises on campus after campus across the country.

to provide needed choice and flexibility; and importantly, in recent years, the mandates of federal law and regulation. In this environment, full-scale benefits program reviews were few and far between on America's campuses. New entitlements and insurance benefits were, far more often than not, simply added to existing plans and programs without consideration of long-term consequences. This golden age of benefits program enhancement ended in the late 1980s as the dark clouds of financial concern turned into full-blown firestorms in budget crises on campus after campus across the country.

The need to manage diminishing resources became a top priority for trustees and administrators as deficits piled on deficits. In this climate, new benefits program initiatives were suspended or canceled as examinations of campus revenues and expenditures became the order of the day.

Campus Budgets

Hard Times

Many emerging trends came together in this late 1980s early 1990s period to adversely affect nearly every college and university in the nation. These included the financial pressures of reduced federal, state, and local support; strong resistance to sharp tuition increases; declining enrollments on some campuses; more restrictive rules for research and indirect cost recoveries; increased competition for grants and contracts; and rapidly increasing operating expenses. These changes and the painfully slow recovery from the recession of 1991-92 have convinced most leaders in higher education that the current hard times will last for at least several more years.

A near universal response has been intensified resource management, which usually begins with easy-to-take actions and progresses to the more difficult as the crisis continues. As the picture of the projected gap between revenues and expenditures becomes clearer, the trustees and administration begin to develop new, or reexamine existing, multiyear budgets. This review frequently results in the announcement and implementation of institution-wide strategic planning and budgeting.

These comprehensive, long-term planning and budgeting approaches occur, perhaps, in as many forms as there are colleges and universities. The common elements of most such strategic reviews are detailed examinations of the multiyear cost and value of all administrative and academic programs projected over three, five, or more years.

It takes a great deal of time and institutional energy to formulate goals and develop and implement a sound strategic planning and budgeting process. For the college or university used to budgeting a year or two at a time with little or no concern about the long-term consequences of program and capital commitments, the transition to a goals-oriented strategic process can be difficult. Even institutions used to multiyear budgeting have found it difficult to develop the understanding, support, and commitment required to reach consensus on a strategic plan to deal with diminished resources.

Resolving a long-term fiscal crisis demands an inordinate amount of time, great skill, and a willingness to hold the course on the part of trustees, the president or chancellor, the deans, the officers, and other academic and administrative leaders. It is not easy work. Results come hard and often at a big price in terms of faculty, staff, alumni, and community relations.

Tough Decisions

The first and easiest current budget cuts or actions to curtail future spending often occur before the strategic review begins or even is contemplated by institutional management. These cuts usually will happen because it is desirable to send an attention-getting message to the campus community. Frequently changes of this nature occur as "freezes" in hiring of staff; across-the-board reductions in current spending authority; limitations or prohibitions on travel; and cancellation or postponement of certain types of purchases.

As the fiscal crisis worsens and the strategic planning process gets underway, these actions may be intensified and supplemented by program reviews that result in current operating budget cuts, program consolidation, and staff reductions. During these phases on most campuses, these program curtailments and staff reductions hit principally nonacademic administrative areas.

It is only much later in the strategic review process that similar actions are proposed in academic programs. Simply put, this delay is recognition of the fact that campus shared governance requires full faculty involvement. Often this means that specific goals for conserving resources cannot be agreed on and the process grinds on slowly or stops completely. Under the best of circumstances it is time consuming and frustrating.

Experience on scores of campuses demonstrates clearly that it is extremely difficult—and sometimes impossible—to reach agreement on academic program and faculty changes even after months of discussion. It is well known that proposing drastic changes, too soon or on too fast a track without the understanding (if not support) and acceptance by the academic community has brought down many a president and administration.

Benefits

Dear to the Heart

It goes almost without saying that, for faculty and staff, a generous benefits program is an essential part of total compensation. Trustees and campus leaders certainly understand and support this view.

College and university benefits budgets generally consist of a complex fabric of plans and programs: some are mandated by law and regulation, some are insurance based, some consist of universal or targeted entitlements. Many are based on long-held traditions unique in the higher education industry.

Each, however, has a long history and all are favored strongly by the campus community of faculty, staff, retirees, and their families. Reaction to any hint of change (much less a proposal for a take-away however small) is always immediate and strong. In such an environment one might expect changes to come slowly.

Take It Slow and Easy

Actions to bring benefits expenditures in line with revised goals evolve in a manner that mirrors the sequence of events in other functional areas. That slow-to-make-changes process might be described as, first, suspending program enhancements (inaction), then attacking easy-to-identify targets (tactical action), and, finally, reducing, consolidating, or eliminating least valued plans and programs (strategic action).

If benefits changes have been discussed regularly, approved, and implemented after an annual review process, an important benefits strategic planning element already may be in place. The type of benefits changes that usually occur as a result of these annual exercises include approval of one or more of the following: increased insurance plan costs, new providers for insurance plans, some small increase in cost-sharing for current faculty and staff, and stricter eligibility rules for new participants. Only rarely will an annual review include any consideration of changes in entitlement benefits such as retirement plans.

It is a formidable task to make major plan and program changes that alter the terms of existing entitlement benefits. Such an effort must be carried out carefully by a broad-based group that fairly represents all campus interests. Therefore, any proposal or external threat that may suggest or require changes in entitlement benefits becomes a priority concern of faculty and staff. Standing committees on benefits or, perhaps, the narrower issues of retirement, are active on many campuses. Ad hoc committees generally are formed to deal with critical current issues such as a fiscal crisis or significant new federal mandates. These committees always involve faculty and, more and more often, staff as well. They often work *quite* slowly.

As a benefits program review—designed to make either a quick hit or to reduce the rate of future growth—gets underway, it is very important to keep in mind the basic difference between entitlement benefits and insurance benefits. Entitlement benefits are used by everyone, insurance benefits only by those with particular wants and needs. It is obvious, therefore, that it is much easier to effect changes in insurance benefits.

As a benefits program review…gets underway it is important to keep in mind the basic difference between entitlement benefits and insurance benefits.

Skyrocketing Costs

Modest increases in benefits costs and rates have been realities in college and university budgets for many years. In the golden age of benefits, these incremental changes received little or no attention in the budget process. Concern about the relative importance, value, and cost of benefits rarely were discussed at the policy-making level. This lack of concern changed as abruptly as skyrocketing costs began to attract attention in the late 1980s. In many colleges and universities benefit costs began to increase at two and sometimes three times the rate of salaries (6 to 10 percent per year versus 3 to 4 percent). It should be noted that institutions that budget on a total compensation basis and assess a single benefits rate on full-time salaries have discovered that this disparity can wreak havoc over time. Under that budgeting approach, rapidly rising benefits costs will affect salary increases adversely quite quickly.

The benefits budget shock was the direct result of two trends that emerged in the 1980s—double digit increases in the cost of institutional health care plans and new burdens imposed by changes in federal law and regulation dealt devastating blows to college and university benefits costs.

The major impact from federal actions came in two areas: from rapidly rising social security and Medicare taxes (while program values fell sharply) and from the Tax Reform Act of 1986 and subsequent legislation that imposed new nondiscrimination requirements and mandated changes in retirement plans. These actions imposed direct and indirect financial and administrative burdens on colleges and universities in taxes, in compliance with law and complex regulations, and by cost-shifting in health care. All of these costs are seen as uncontrollable except to the extent that employment is curtailed.

Rising health care costs have been especially painful. The year after year run-up in these costs and the resulting crisis have been the center of national public policy attention for some time. Campus budget, human resource, and benefits officers have been aware of and concerned about these trends for several years. Benefits budgets have been hit hard by health care plan cost increases, yet most colleges and universities have avoided draconian actions to control these costs.

Most American industries that fight the health care cost containment battle are seen as being in a losing situation except for all but the largest, toughest, and often most desperate employer. Unions generally have made health benefits their top priority and as a result, bitter—and almost always successful—strikes have been called to prevent loss of benefits.

It comes as no surprise, therefore, that college and university policy makers have been unwilling to brutalize faculty and staff in the course of their struggle to balance the need to maintain excellent benefits with efforts to control costs. However, most institutions have taken some actions to limit or share costs while at the same time reducing plan inequities. Many of these approaches have been targeted, onetime efforts to achieve limited objectives; others have been in the form of flexible benefits programs that encourage desired behavior by offering broad plan choice, pricing differentials, and tax advantages.

Despite these efforts, many campus leaders are not satisfied they have done enough or, for that matter, that they *can* do enough to keep cost increases within reason. As a result, many are discouraged and have conceded that, in their real world, health care and other benefits costs are all but uncontrollable.

Exploring the Universe

Despite the high value of benefits to faculty and staff, and the intractable nature of their rising costs, it makes sense and it usually is necessary to examine each and every benefits plan and program when an institution-wide planning and budgeting review is undertaken in a time of fiscal crisis.

A full-scale benefits program review is neither easy nor trouble-free. Some in fact have been disastrous. But, depending on the understanding of the triggering crisis, the goals articulated, and the effectiveness of the methods used to get support, satisfactory results can be achieved without undue acrimony.

The tasks required to complete a successful comprehensive benefits review will resemble strongly the list that follows: identify and report the problem; get approval of goal or goals and time for completion; organize the review staff and mobilize resources; define the parameters of the work; identify plan features, funding, costs, and options for change; develop a firm time and task schedule; prepare a report of findings and possible actions; listen carefully to faculty and staff concerns; present recommendations for final approval; communicate approved changes and schedule implementation; and, finally, evaluate and report results.

It is essential to establish and maintain effective communications with the campus community at every step in the process.

It is essential to establish and maintain effective communications with the campus community at every step in the process. Community awareness, understanding, and support are vital to ensure the best possible outcome—a carefully designed and executed two-way communications effort provides the guarantee of acceptance, if not full approval, of what may be bitter medicine for faculty and staff.

Stop, Look, and Listen

Any benefits review that does not recognize campus-specific tradition, recent history, and current climate often will be doomed before it begins. The process for conducting a full-scale or nearly full-scale benefits review necessarily must be modified to conform to the unique philosophy, policies, and governance practices of the college or university involved.

No review should be undertaken unless the problem is defined clearly and firm, time-framed goals have been discussed thoroughly and accepted by trustees and academic and administrative leaders. Faculty and staff benefits are too important and far too sensitive to be dealt with cavalierly.

Unless there is clear evidence the benefits budget is in trouble and there are plans that are not performing well, it is better not to undertake a review. Action usually is necessary, however, to deal with runaway costs in key plans, abuse or major problems in others, and, in some cases, circumstances that have obsoleted plans or made them unfair or illegal. While it is beyond the scope of this chapter to list the scores of situations that might be deemed "important and urgent" for attention in a given institution, the message should be clear—proceed with caution.

Getting the Job Done

Step by Step

A benefits review can and should be flexible. There are, however, essential elements that must be in place. The initial fact finding must be complete and indisputable; and the goal or goals, project leadership, communications approach, and time for approval and implementation must be agreed on and supported through "hell and high water" by institutional leadership. With these basics in mind the step-by-step process can be described in the following manner.

Identify and Report the Problem. The first news of an emerging major problem comes from the benefits, human resource, or budget officer after examination of the annual benefits program expenditures and projections for the next three or more years. When major deviations from budget or changes in projected expenditures or benefits rates are confirmed, disclosure and detailed discussions with the chief financial officer usually follow. If the evidence is compelling, the findings and conclusions, perhaps with recommendations, are brought to the president and his academic and administrative colleagues for review and discussion. It is at this point that the pros and cons of various moves should be considered and final recommendations for trustee and/or administrative actions are formulated.

Get Approval of Goal or Goals and Time for Completion. Trustees and institutional leaders should set clear goals for the work and a specific time for implementation. This statement of expectations is of immense help as the process moves forward. Highest level approval of the review and its goals is an irresistible force in the struggle with those who want to delay change if an implementation schedule is mandated at the outset.

Organize the Review Staff and Mobilize Resources. The best way to ensure on time results for a well defined, tightly time-framed project is management by a small high-level group led by a strong individual who is well-known and respected by the community. The members of this group must be available for frequent, regular, and on-the-fly meetings and must make this work their highest priority. Resources also must be available— detailed plan analysis, descriptions of options, cost projections, suggestions for communications—all may require help of institutional staff and outside experts.

Define the Parameters of the Work. An early identification of what is on the table and what is not is important to expedite the work and build the credibility of the review. Even though the charge to the group may call for "a full-scale review of benefits plans and programs," it frequently is prudent to suggest excluding some plans from review—social security and Medicare taxes come quickly to mind. Unemployment and workers' compensation costs and vacation accruals, if relevant, are other issues that may be set aside at least in the first stage of the work.

Other issues that should be dealt with—sooner or later— may be what emphasis to put on "cost reduction" versus "cost sharing" versus "cost avoidance," willingness to restrict freedom of choice, willingness to end long-term relationships with local providers, degree of application to all faculty and staff, and ability to use "carrot and stick" techniques to achieve desired results. Obviously, this list can be long!

Correctly classifying objectives as impossible, difficult, and relatively easy to achieve usually is not part of this early work.

However, recognizing that faculty and staff, or institutional leadership, will not accept one type of solution may well lead to a trade-off that makes another easier to accept. Finding the way to success means avoiding, but recognizing and discussing, real roadblocks and negotiating a favorable solution however rough it may be along the way.

Identify Plan Features, Funding, Costs, and Options. Staff must gather and be prepared to present relevant information about each plan in the benefits program. At a minimum the data should include a complete description of the current benefit; the funding (where the money goes—to individuals, insurance companies, other providers and suppliers, internal departments, etc.); actual and projected year-by-year costs; significant changes in the last five years in plan design, benefits, or providers; and, finally, detail on options for changes and savings that are possible.

Preparing these information sheets—of no more than two pages in a standard format—is time consuming work but it is critical. These data sheets are the building blocks for a well-structured report of findings.

Develop a Detailed Time and Task Schedule. To comply with the mandate—for time-certain implementation of benefits changes to meet institutional goals—a project time and task schedule must be constructed with great care. It must be understood, accepted, and approved by institutional leaders early in the process. This schedule, with its soft and hard deadlines for various actions, must be made known to the campus community as recommendations for benefits changes are discussed.

If the basic problem has been well defined and the need for prompt resolution is seen, no delay in implementation should be tolerated. A right-and-tight time and task schedule should minimize conflict and ensure timely implementation.

Prepare a Report of Findings and Possible Actions. The staff report should be presented as promptly as possible to administrative, academic, and key faculty leadership; it should be amended as necessary, and approved before general discussion with faculty and staff groups begins. The revised report—with its clear identification of optional approaches to the solution of the benefits budget problem—can then be communicated widely in all possible campus media or, preferably, become the basis for extensive discussions with individuals

Finding the way to success means avoiding, but recognizing and discussing, real roadblocks and negotiating a favorable solution however rough it may be along the way.

and groups of faculty and staff.

Listen Carefully to Faculty and Staff Concerns. Every possible effort must be made to listen to the views of faculty and staff. Reductions in the value or increases in the costs of benefits will not come easily.

Pretesting reactions, by working from a statement of desired outcomes, is a technique that has worked well in many environments. There are many ways to do this. For example, the form may be based on one or all of the following: a statement of principles drawn up by a campuswide group of faculty leaders, a report from staff focus groups, or a statement of goals for benefits developed earlier.

As optional approaches to the resolution of a benefits budget crisis are reviewed and discussed in open forums or with standing or ad hoc committees of faculty and staff, great care should be taken by task force leaders to explain the situation fully and respond candidly and accurately to all comments and questions. At this point in the process it should be made clear that action will be taken and at a specific time. The purpose of the meetings is to develop understanding, solicit opinions on preferences, and encourage all participants to express their views. Many constructive views will surface. There will, of course, be some outright expression of distrust, unfairness, frustration and anger—it is a natural part of the process.

Present Recommendations for Review and Approval. With the listening step completed it usually will be quite easy to formulate the recommendations for change. It is unusual not to have a strong consensus at this point. The course of action will not be liked by many, but it will be understood and accepted by most. It should be approved as quickly as possible and announced immediately thereafter.

Communicate Approved Changes and Schedule Implementation. The decisions reached at the end of the long benefits review process must be communicated carefully and implemented on schedule. In most institutions changes will be scheduled to take effect on either January 1 (to coincide with benefits that relate to certain statutes or plan years) or at the start of the fiscal year (frequently July 1). If the time and task calendar has been adhered to, the implementation ordinarily will proceed smoothly.

Evaluate and Report Results of Actions Taken. Benefits and human resource staff should monitor and report soon after implementation and periodically thereafter on the effect of the program changes. The reports should include opinions and anecdotal data about staff attitudes as well as the specifics of savings realized. This step is important in an environment where further examination of the benefits budget is likely to occur.

As the actual results of the exercise become known—usually after the close of the first fiscal year, when the impact of the changes is fully evident—institutional leadership should get a report complete with new multiyear projections that compare the "before and after" situation.

A special report on actions *not* taken also may be in order. The benefits review is likely to uncover a number of opportunities for savings and significant plan deficiencies—especially in entitlement benefits—that require further evaluation before action is possible.

From Discovery to Decision in Less than a Year

As stated earlier in this chapter, the process described in the preceding pages is structured to produce results quickly and effectively. The work, from discovery and reporting of the problem to final approval of action, can be completed in less than a year (from two and a half months after the close of one fiscal year to one month after the start of the next).

Many readers will say this cannot be done. It is easy to agree that this is *not* the usual experience in higher education. It is well known that many such exercises go on for months or years with no positive measurable results, but rest assured, if the need is great and the will is strong, it can and will be done. In concept this fast-track process dovetails perfectly with other urgent institutional efforts to bring balance between revenues and expenditures; in practice, if done with care, it will be accepted and will cause only minimal damage to faculty and staff relations.

7

Total Quality Management Principles and Strategic Planning

Deborah J. Teeter and G. Gregory Lozier

Browsing through the business section of any bookstore one is assaulted by a myriad of titles that espouse various concepts and tools to ensure business success. Many of these ideas eventually make their way into the management practices of higher education institutions. For example, since the early 1980s, many colleges and universities have been exploring strategic planning concepts and practices to better position themselves for the future. More recently, some higher education institutions are finding the principles of Total Quality Management (TQM) appealing as consumers become more outspoken in their demand for quality and value. This chapter talks about the origins of TQM, describes its principles and concepts, and discusses the links with strategic and Hoshin (or "target") planning. This chapter shares the principles of TQM and indicates its alignment with planning.

In the Beginning...

At the turn of the century, a British researcher named R. A. Fisher was studying ways to improve crop production. Recognizing the limitations imposed by the growing season on experiments, he sought other methods to explore the effect of various seed depths, watering, and the use of fertilizer on production enhancement. He utilized statistical methods to sort through mounds of data quickly to identify key cause-and-effect relationships. The quality movement and the field of statistics in general are outgrowths of his research during the first two decades of this century (Port and Carey, 1991).[1]

Fisher's work caught the attention of Walter A. Shewhart, a physicist working at Western Electric (now AT&T) Bell Laboratories. By the 1930s Shewhart transformed these various statistical concepts into a discipline to improve quality control in factories (Port and Carey, 1991).[2] These statistical methods and structured problem-solving techniques were critical in developing telephone technology. The reliable phone service enjoyed today harkens back to early research done at Bell Labs using these statistical tools and methods.

W. Edwards Deming, a statistician, began working for Western Electric in the mid-1920s and mentored with and was influenced by Shewhart and his thinking. Later, Deming worked for the U.S. Census Bureau and, in the late 1940s, helped American occupation forces determine the Japanese population using statistical sampling techniques (Dobyns and Crawford-Mason, 1991).[3]

During World War II Deming and others developed a new philosophy of quality from statistical techniques to improve American war materials (Dobyns and Crawford-Mason, 1991).[4] Statistical process control techniques were critical to ensure armaments would function as expected since it was impossible to "test" every bullet.

Statistical process control techniques became highly developed during the war effort to ensure high quality products. After World War II, those same techniques were peddled to American business executives. However, these leaders exhibited little interest since the market for American goods, regardless of quality, was flourishing and quantity was in demand.

To help rebuild Japan so United States occupation would not be necessary, Deming, Joseph Juran, and others were brought to Japan to revive the Japanese economy using the same statistical techniques that ensured quality armaments during the war. Products stamped "Made in Japan" were of inferior quality and languished in the marketplace. The Japanese were not in a position to protest the efforts to improve product quality. The results of those efforts are evident today in the high quality products produced by Japan and their effect on world markets. To recognize the role these quality initiatives played in the redevelopment of Japan's economy, the Japanese Union of Scientists and Engineers established in 1951 the annual Deming Prize to recognize and stimulate continuous improvement.

Over the past half century, Deming developed and refined a management philosophy that stemmed from his initial work in statistical process control. Major elements of this philosophy are contained in his 14 points regarding management's obligations, listed in Exhibit 1. In these principles, Deming presents his quality ideas regarding constancy of purpose, customer satisfaction, systematic analysis, total costs, workplace fear, and human resource development. From these beginnings, a management philosophy has evolved that was reintroduced to American business in 1980 with the airing of an NBC documentary titled "If Japan Can...Why Can't We?" An economic war is being waged and as American businesses adopt quality principles and concepts, the challenge now is, "if business can...why can't education?"

What Is Quality?

Ask any group or individual how to define quality and they are likely to use descriptors such as: reliability; value; affordability; style of presentation; performance; responsiveness; timely; courtesy.

Three proponents recognized for their significant contributions to quality improvement developments offer these definitions:

1. Quality is "fitness for use, as judged by the user."[5] (Juran, 1989)

2. Quality is "conforming to requirements."[6] (Crosby, 1984)

3. Quality is "surpassing customer needs and expectations."[7] (Gitlow, 1987)

Exhibit 1
W. Edward Deming's Management Obligations

1. Create constancy of purpose for the improvement of product and service, with the aim to become competitive and to stay in business, and to provide jobs.
2. Adopt the new philosophy. We are in a new economic age. Western management must awaken to the challenge, must learn their responsibilities, and take on leadership for change.
3. Cease dependence on inspection to achieve quality. Eliminate the need for inspection on a mass basis by building quality into the product in the first place.
4. End the practice of awarding business on the basis of price tag. Instead, minimize total cost. Move toward a single supplier for any one item, on a long-term relationship of loyalty and trust.
5. Improve constantly and forever the system of production and service, to improve quality and productivity, and thus constantly decrease costs.
6. Institute training on the job.
7. Institute leadership. The aim of supervision should be to help people and machines and gadgets to do a better job. Supervision of management is in need of overhaul, as well as supervision of production workers.
8. Drive out fear, so everyone may work effectively for the company.
9. Break down barriers between departments. People in research, design, sales, and production must work as a team, to foresee problems of production and in use that may be encountered with the product or service.
10. Eliminate slogans, exhortations, and targets for the work force asking for zero defects and new levels of productivity. Such exhortations only create adversarial relationships, as the bulk of the causes of low quality and low productivity belong to the system and thus lie beyond the power of the work force.
11. Eliminate work standards (quotas) on the factory floor. Substitute leadership. Eliminate management by objective. Eliminate management by numbers and numerical goals. Substitute leadership.
12. Remove barriers that rob the hourly worker of his right to pride of workmanship. The responsibility of supervisors must be changed from sheer numbers to quality. Remove barriers that rob people in management and in engineering of their right to pride of workmanship. This means, inter alia, abolishment of the annual or merit rating and of management by objective.
13. Institute a vigorous program of education and self-improvement.
14. Put everybody in the organization to work to accomplish the transformation. The transformation is everybody's job.

Whether explicit or implicit, the concept of customer underlies each of these definitions. Further, customer includes both external and internal "beneficiaries." Internal beneficiaries include coworkers and entire units that serve one another within an organization. The principle these TQM gurus espouse is that customers define quality.

About 10 years ago in an article in the *Educational Record* titled "Quality—Indefinable But Not Unattainable," Harold Enarson (1983) former President of Ohio State University stated that "quality is something we know in our bones."[8] More recently, David Garvin (1988) wrote about "transcendent quality" in which the purveyor of quality is likely to observe that "I know it when I see it."[9] Such attitudes about quality are typical in higher education. Many at colleges and universities claim they know intrinsically when quality is present but few are willing to define it. Similarly, faculty and administrators alike are reluctant to call students, or anyone else, a "customer." In this environment, strong objections are presented to the language, principles, and methods of TQM.

But consider the following: Should students expect to graduate in four years? Should students be able to tell a faculty member that material in last Wednesday's class was unclear? What is a reasonable time period for being reimbursed for institution travel (perhaps before the credit card statement arrives)? What do final exams contribute if teaching-learning feedback is provided throughout the term? Should students have to go to five different offices to withdraw from a course? How can an institution's reclassification process more effectively contribute to human resource development? Should all inquiries about employment opportunities receive the courtesy of an acknowledgment? Should job applicants following an interview be informed of the likely date of further notification of their status? Does a requisition for a $15 laboratory supplies purchase really need three signatures?

Developing answers to these questions and responding to concerns about the applicability of TQM to higher education require addressing issues such as employee expectations; human interrelationships; understanding how work gets done; trust, or lack thereof; and the cost of increased bureaucracy and complexity that results from abuse by a few.

Colleges and universities interested in improving their responses to these questions must face change, important change, in the way they look and think about themselves and the way they function. That change focuses on the pursuit of quality. The principles of TQM are neither new nor unique. What is new, however, is a greater recognition that institutions can and must pursue quality consciously through systematic means.

Foundations of TQM for Higher Education

The foundations for TQM operate in concert with one another. They are symbiotic and synergistic. All foundations must be in place for an organization to truly realize the promise TQM holds for providing quality outputs, services, and experiences. These foundations are: mission/vision; customer focus; process improvements; systematic analysis; collaboration; and systems thinking.

Establishing a Mission—Creating a Vision

Understanding and improving quality requires knowing what we do, our purpose as an organization. The first of Deming's 14 points for management is to "create constancy of purpose." Constancy of purpose requires persistence and a long-term commitment to a well-established and understood mission statement that provides an organization with a framework to make decisions in a consistent manner. Gitlow and Gitlow (1987) observed that "The process of (1) developing a mission statement, (2) making it a living document, and (3) socializing new employees to the mission statement is what is needed to begin the 'journey to quality.'"[10] It is this commitment to purpose that provides the motivation for long-term change.

Closely aligned with mission are organizational values. Values express the "moral character" of an institution. They help direct an institution's policy and decisions on matters such as individual diversity, intellectual freedom, portfolio investiture, and freedom of speech, among others. Organizational values are both enabling and challenging and facilitate the interaction of individually held values with corporate values.

If mission is knowing the answer to "what" an organization does and values express "who" the institution is, vision tells "where" the organization is going. A vision statement describes what the organization will be like when its mission and goals are achieved. The vision declares what the organization wants to become; it can mean doing more or being different, but it most certainly should mean being better. Without a vision, the college, university, or individual unit within the quality-focused institution is less likely to advance or improve.

Focusing on the Customer

According to Collins and Porras (1991) a statement of purpose also conveys "how the organization fills basic human needs...and plays an essential role in determining who's inside and who's outside the organization."[11] An organization must identify not only what it does, but also the individuals or groups—the customers—it serves. Knowing who receives the benefits of teaching, research, and service becomes a requisite to quality enhancement. Building on the three definitions of quality cited earlier, and in thinking about their customers, all institutions should answer questions about whose use, whose requirements, and whose needs and expectations they are serving.

Colleges and universities, through both primary functions and the full array of supporting services, serve a broad range of customers, both within and outside the institution. These customers include employees, students, parents, government officials, business and industry, alumni, and funding agencies. Focusing on the customer's needs requires learning what those needs are and then meeting them.

Improving the Process Continuously

Processes—the flow of work activities—are the means by which the organization carries out its mission. Traditionally, much attention is paid to inputs (for example, test scores of entering students, the number of faculty members with doctorates, the number of books in the library, or the budget of the institution), design (for example, curricula, research proposals, benefits programs, human resource information systems designs), and outputs (for example, number of graduates, number of graduates employed, training programs offered, or personnel applications processed). However, institutions give far less attention to the means—the academic support, and administrative support processes—used to deliver and support instruction, research, and service. Among the common macrolevel processes at colleges and universities are, for example: teaching-learning; advising; grant proposal/development; orientation; research investigation; registration; library book circulation; testing-evaluation; grade processing; payroll; admissions; purchasing; curriculum development; and staff recruitment (faculty hiring).

Delving more deeply into an academic process such as faculty hiring might uncover the following subprocesses: authorization to fill the position; advertising the position; processing applications; setting up interviews; selection process; and offer process.

Pursuing improvements in the quality of these subprocesses and processes requires eliminating or reducing process waste. By focusing on subprocesses of complex processes, it is easier to identify the waste. There are three types of process waste: rework, scrap, and unnecessary complexity. Rework is fixing earlier mistakes. It is taking a course over again, repeating material not adequately covered in a course prerequisite, redrafting a check originally issued in the wrong amount, or redoing prospective employee interviews because of asking illegal questions. Scrap is work that is discarded and begun over again. It is staff terminations and aborted faculty searches, students flunking out, committee recommendations ignored, and planning processes abandoned. Unnecessary complexity is taking steps that add no value to the process. It is too many signatures on an employee change-of-status form, endless steps in a leave approval process, three different forms to apply for overseas travel, and elaborate justifications to purchase equipment. All of these examples of rework, scrap, and unnecessary complexity could be characterized as process defects. Ultimately, process improvement comes not from detecting these defects—for example, through testing at the end of a course to determine whether a student knows the subject matter and passes the course—but rather from preventing defects, that is, by using systematic analysis to determine whether the subject matter is being presented adequately (taught) and received (learned).

Using Systematic Analysis

"In God we trust. All others must use data." This remark, often attributed to Deming, conveys the importance of data and analysis for the pursuit of quality. As discussed earlier in this chapter, TQM has its roots in statistical quality control of the 1920s, 1930s, and 1940s. Organizations now use statistics increasingly to model processes and determine ways to improve both process and output. Thus, TQM places considerable emphasis on the scientific method, or what Shewhart termed the plan-do-check-act (PDCA) cycle (Sherr and Lozier, 1991), described in Table 1.

Table 1
PDCA Cycle

Plan: Identify a process in need of improvement, analyze the problems, and develop a proposal for change that will cause some type of improvement.

Do: Run an experiment with the proposed change.

Check: Collect data to determine if the experiment produced the desired change.

Act: If the experiment is successful, implement the idea more broadly; if not, learn from the mistake and try an alternative.[12]

In addition to being systematic, the scientific method also requires the institution to base changes on fact rather than on conjecture or innuendo. Several fundamental but relatively unsophisticated statistical tools can help one understand processes and analyze data about processes. These tools include flowcharts, cause-and-effect diagrams, Pareto charts, checklists, histograms, scatter diagrams, and run and control charts. The purposes of collecting data and analyzing it statistically are to identify where variation exists in a process and what causes it.

Understanding the role of variation is fundamental to the pursuit of quality and systematic analysis. Variation exists in every process. There are two types of variation: special causes and common causes. Special causes arise from unique circumstances; they are not part of normal functioning. Special causes create abnormal variation or surprises in the process. The first step in process improvement is to identify a special cause and eliminate it from consideration—by actually eliminating the possibility of the cause happening in the future, by devising contingency operations in the event it or a similar cause does recur in the future, or by recognizing the total uniqueness of the cause and understanding that it will not affect the normal operations of a process and the ability to improve it. For example, tracking the causes of errors in payroll check processing and amounts may indicate when problems are created by unique circumstances or are the result of normal procedures. Examples of special events that might cause payroll checks to be late include, for example, an electrical outage that disrupts the computer processing of checks, an influenza outbreak among the staff at a critical time, or a major winter storm that keeps payroll clerks from work. In analyzing the special cases, one may respond to the first case by installing a backup generator to address the electrical outage; in the second case, cross-train staff with another department to provide backup in emergencies (or develop a relationship with an outside contractor to provide staff on call that have been trained and used periodically to cover absences); and in the third case, recognize that acts of nature are beyond control and "suppress that data point" in the analysis. These are examples of special causes in a support process that can create aberrations in the process and its intended effects. Continuous improvement in the quality of this payroll process first requires dealing with these special causes.

Common causes are inherent in the process, occur regularly over time, affect everyone working in the process, and affect all outcomes of the process. Many such causes create rework, scrap, and unnecessary complexity. The second step in process improvement is to identify and reduce variation from common causes through careful, databased, permanent changes in the process. For example, fewer errors in the administration of benefits might result from improved training of personnel directing new employees how to complete the benefits application form. Reducing the time required for physical plant repairs could mean carrying the parts most frequently needed on the repair truck rather than withdrawing them from general stores each time they are needed. If data indicate that completing homework assignments enhances learning, fewer students might flunk the course if measures are developed to promote doing homework.

A process without special causes is "in control," that is, it is stable and predictable. Once a process is in control, quality improvement-based steps can be undertaken to reduce the variation arising from common causes.

Promoting Collaboration

Teamwork and team decision making are important aspects of quality process improvement. So, why teams? To improve processes requires the involvement of those most familiar with the process because who better knows how to improve the process than those who understand the process, are involved in the process, and desire to improve the process. Processes operating or confined to a single organizational unit would be improved by a team composed of members from that organization. Other processes may transcend organizational boundaries and require members from several areas to form a cross-functional team. Teams must work in partnership with managers who have the authority to implement process improvement changes proposed by the team. Administrators are critical collaborators in the process improvement cycle. They "sponsor" teams, approve process improvement initiatives, and provide guidelines or constraints regarding acceptable solutions. Sponsors must be committed to implementing solutions proposed by teams that meet specified guidelines/constraints.

Collaboration requires empowerment—an atmosphere where people feel comfortable, confident, motivated, and responsible for conducting their work. Members of a team share responsibility and credit for the team's decisions and accomplishments. Collaboration recognizes that the people most intimately involved in a process understand best how it functions and how to improve it. Collaboration also focuses on the way in which things get done, not on blaming workers for failures or defects.

When 80 percent of the students cannot clearly see the experiment being demonstrated, it does not improve quality to tell students not to miss the laboratory class. Exhorting employees to "work faster" will not shorten the time required to process student registrations. Providing too few sections of a required course will not increase student satisfaction with advising. Unless the organization collaborates with the participants, it is unlikely to understand a process well enough to improve it.

Higher education lags significantly behind the corporate sector in its attention to ongoing human resource training and development. Yet colleges and universities are in the business of education and their functions are human resource intensive. Quality improvement requires that people know how to do their jobs—how to advise, how to teach, how to do research, how to process a form, and how to handle telephone inquiries. They need to know how their job relates to jobs that others do and how their functions contribute to the mission.

In a quality organization, teamwork becomes standard operating procedure and employee collaboration becomes part of the organizational culture. Use of teams is one means of promoting collaboration. Structured teams can be instrumental in helping individuals understand the principles of focusing on the customer, systematic analysis, and continuous improvement.

At some colleges and universities, teams have examined particular processes such as physical plant renovations, disposition of hazardous waste, recovery of sponsored research funding, processing financial pledges, faculty hiring, freshmen orientation and advising, human resource office telephone response time, and the learning of physics by engineering students. However, if special teams become the only means by which the organization pursues quality, the prospect of achieving continuous improvement is diminished greatly. According to Scholtes and others, special teams can become dysfunctional if they communicate that quality improvement is a separate function outside one's normal work relationships and responsibilities.[13] In a transformed organization, the pursuit of quality is a way of life that is not limited to activities associated with special teams.

In a quality organization, teamwork becomes standard operating procedure and employee collaboration becomes part of the organizational culture.

Recognizing the Institution as a System

An overriding principle of TQM is systems thinking. Senge (1990) calls this the fifth discipline and says it serves as the foundation of "the learning organization."[14] According to Senge, a learning organization "is a place where people are continually discovering how they create their reality."[15] The learning organization constantly expands its capacity to create the future and achieves this goal by recognizing that the success of any individual depends on the success of others.

With respect to the pursuit of quality and TQM, systems thinking reinforces the need to recognize the interrelationships among people, processes, design, and materials. Exhibit 2 portrays the institution as a system of continuous improvement. At the heart of the system are the core processes of teaching, learning, research, and service. These are supported by a variety of academic and administrative services. People, materials, and resources are the inputs to these processes, as supplied by other education sectors, funding agencies, and governmental entities. The institution's core processes generate outputs—educated graduates, research, and services performed—for the institution's diverse customers and beneficiaries. Driving components of both process design and improvement are the needs, expectations, and feedback provided by the customers. Overlaying the entire system are the mission and values of the institution that provide direction. Finally, underlying the system is comprehensive, systematic analysis to provide the data and information necessary to inform continuous improvement.

Systems thinking means that an institution cannot improve the learning process unless it works with the students who are doing the learning; it cannot improve purchasing response time without involving the departments making the purchases; it cannot improve information systems without interviewing those who use the systems hardware and software. Systems thinking says that faculty who have a higher instructional load contribute to the success of faculty who conduct cutting-edge, funded research and teach less.

Ingredients for Creating a Total Quality Environment

An understanding of the conceptual foundations of TQM is necessary to the pursuit of TQM but insufficient for them to take hold in an organization. Leadership, commitment, and persistence are also essential ingredients for TQM to flourish.

Leadership. Selznick (1957) has observed that a major function of effective leadership "is the creation of conditions that will make possible in the future what is excluded in the present."[16] Leadership is both acclaimed for the success and blamed for the failure of organizations. Expectations of leaders are high and, as with all critical endeavors of an organization, leadership plays a key role in the pursuit of TQM by an organization.

The principles of TQM are not an esoteric set of principles

Exhibit 2

THE UNIVERSITY AS A SYSTEM OF CONTINUOUS IMPROVEMENT

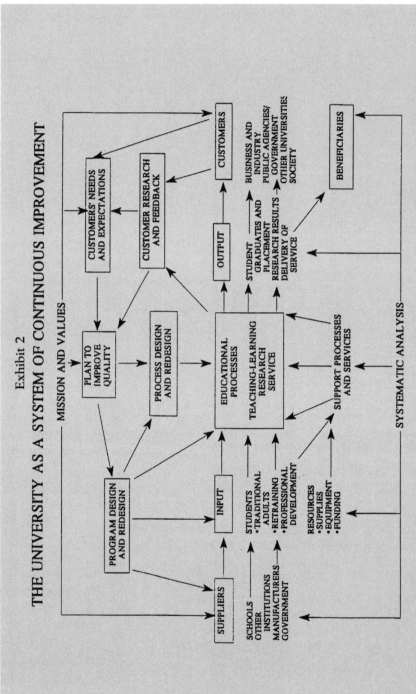

Adapted from *Out of the Crisis*, page 4, by W. Edwards Deming. Published by MIT Center for Advanced Engineering Study, Cambridge, MA 02139. Copyright 1986 by W. Edwards Deming. Reprinted by permission of MIT and The W. Edward Deming Institute.

to guide an organization; rather the concepts provide a basis for the daily operation of an organization. An organization with a focus on quality constantly is asking a series of questions about every activity that it conducts: What is the purpose of the activity? Whom does it serve? How well does it serve? What evidence do we have of its performance? How can it be improved continually? Leaders of institutions that pursue TQM need to create an environment that enables people at all levels to ask these and similar questions. Challenging the status quo needs to be not only tolerated but also encouraged. It is not change for the sake of change, but change for the improvement in the quality of an organization's products, services, and experiences. People are less opposed to change than to being changed. Involvement in asking and answering questions about quality makes change agents of everyone.

Studies indicate that between 85 to 94 percent of problems encountered in business are process based, not people based.

Part of enabling change to happen is focusing on what is wrong—the process—rather than who is wrong. Studies indicate that between 85 to 94 percent of problems encountered in business are process based, not people based. This is a cultural shift for many in the United States as evidenced by the importance of placing blame when mishaps occur or problems are experienced. When the Chicago River flooded downtown tunnels and office buildings in 1991, it became quickly evident that city leadership deemed it more important to find someone to blame for the problem than to seek to identity the failures in the process that allowed the tragedy to occur.

Commitment. Also key to creating an atmosphere for improvement is the willingness to acknowledge there are problems. The glib remark "there is always room for improvement" is not the same as formally acknowledging problems and deliberately setting about to address them. A proactive commitment to seek opportunities to improve rather than react to crisis is the hallmark of a quality organization.

Persistence. To realize quality there must be persistence in the pursuit. The journey to becoming a quality organization is not a six-month, one-year, or even two-year transition. Despite the commonsense nature of the principles of TQM, after years of not adhering to such common sense, it is difficult to change overnight the manner in which an organization thinks about and does things. Representatives of corporate entities and higher education institutions such as Motorola, Samford

University, and Fox Valley Technical College all attest to the long-term persistence that is necessary to embrace the principles and practices of quality organization wide.

Alignment of TQM and Strategic Planning Concepts

The principles of TQM are related closely to many of the tenets of strategic planning. To provide a framework for examining the alignment of the concepts, there are several key elements that provide the foundations of strategic planning.

Key Elements of Strategic Planning

Among the key strategic planning concepts presented in Chapter 1 are process, assessment, and leadership/decision making.

Process. First and foremost, strategic planning is a process. That process includes the determination of an organization's mission, goals, and objectives, as well as the establishment of a set of measures by which the organization can test the achievement of those goals and objectives. Strategic planning principles urge broad participation, often realized by extensive use of committees.

Assessment. Strategic planning requires that the institution understand its strengths and weaknesses and assess the external environment so it can position itself to take advantage of available opportunities or defend itself against external threats. Effective assessment requires good data and the development of sound information.

Leadership and Decision Making. Strategic planning requires an advocate—a champion to ensure the translation of plans into decisions. To be fully effective, institutional planning must be integrated into all levels of management of the institution. Those institutions that successfully integrate strategic planning with decision making throughout the institution are likely to have a significant competitive advantage in the future.

Cross-Functional Planning. Frequent inhibitors of successful planning are organizational silos and an institution's inability to plan for issues that transcend these organizational boundaries. Cross-functional planning, although not a core planning concept, is one means to overcome this deficiency and assure that the operational activities of the units support strategic plans.

The Convergence of Total Quality Management and Strategic Planning

The role of mission, the focus on process, and the use of information to guide activities are several areas in which TQM and strategic planning concepts converge. Both also use group processes to determine and implement activities, but the focus and role of the groups are somewhat different. The following section discusses these complementary aspects of TQM and strategic planning.

Mission Driven. Strategic planning and TQM both are mission driven and recognize the critical importance of defining an organization's purpose. Application of TQM principles helps to further refine this purpose by requiring the organization to identify clearly those who are served by the organization and their needs. A mission statement that establishes the identity of the customer facilitates the understanding of the needs to be addressed by the organization.

Process Oriented. Process is central to both strategic planning and TQM. To many, the most crucial aspect of strategic planning is the value achieved through the interaction of the participants, the improved understanding of the organization, the setting of direction, and finally the effect of decisions implemented. In the absence of these elements of process, the written plan is artificial. TQM is both a means to evaluate processes as well as a process itself. TQM is characterized by teamwork, systematic analysis, and use of information to achieve the objective of continuous improvement. TQM can be used to evaluate the strategic planning process itself, to assist in the assessment and evaluation of strategic planning, and to provide a structure by which the goals and objectives of strategic planning can be implemented by focusing on the processes of work.

Information Driven. Both strategic planning and TQM use data to develop, implement, and evaluate plans and to improve processes continuously. TQM can reinforce planning by using structured measurement and by enhancing the availability of objective and quantifiable data as part of the PDCA cycle.

Group Processes. Both strategic planning and TQM involve individuals throughout an organization to shape and execute its activities. However, those who are involved and the way in which they are involved may differ. Strategic planning often relies on committees for advice on policy making and goal setting with implementation taking place in the relevant individual operational units. The committees usually are composed of institutional executives with representatives of the faculty and student body. Problems can emerge if the committees do not include those who actually will implement the change or perform the work. In contrast, TQM posits the use of teams composed of individuals who share ownership in the process being planned or improved. Ownership includes both beneficiaries of the process as well as providers of the process.

Hoshin Planning and TQM

Individuals further exploring the strategic planning-TQM relationship are likely to come across the phrase "Hoshin planning." Hoshin is a Japanese term that loosely translated means target. McCloskey and Collett (1993) describe an organization's Hoshins as issues that are most urgent and critical that flow from long-term (five years) planning processes. "A Hoshin item is an issue or problem which has a relatively short projected time frame for resolution, as a general rule, one year or less, and has a high potential impact on the organization."[17] The authors further suggest that progress toward the Hoshins should be evaluated quarterly with the implications that organizational processes are modified to ensure the organization is moving toward the accomplishment of its Hoshins.

Hoshin planning frequently is linked with TQM initiatives since it provides specific direction for process improvement efforts. Some may see it as a natural extension of other planning efforts and could argue that Hoshin and strategic planning are different sides of the same coin. Both are forward looking as implied by the word "planning." Whether Hoshin planning is viewed as a technique under the larger planning umbrella or as a guiding force, the key notion is that planning activities, however they are labeled, are a critical factor in the practice of TQM.

TQM Role for Human Resource Organizations

Human resource organizations can be a key player in institutions involved with TQM. With any management endeavor, there are functional, operational, and strategic roles to be played. For the human resource department, the functional roles might include training, at an operational level it may be coordinating campus efforts, and on a strategic level it may be to provide a leadership and/or planning role. The human resource department also may be called on to provide human resource data for teams pursuing process improvements in areas where human resource data are essential.

The continuum of roles the human resource department may play in an organization pursuing quality may range from a leadership role to no role. The established role the human resource department already plays in an institution may initially position the role human resources plays in a quality initiative. Movement along the continuum will be enhanced by practicing the principles of TQM within the human resource organization.

A natural role for many human resource organizations to play may be in TQM training. As always, an organization providing training on a particular topic will enhance the credibility of the training by practicing what is being taught.

This can be a tall order. It is much easier to talk about TQM than to do it. To do it requires an understanding of the principles and concepts, a commitment to practice them, and patience for them to affect the organization. Not surprisingly, those identified with a quality initiative often are held to a higher standard of conduct. Training quickly can be rendered ineffective if the principles being taught are not practiced.

A natural role for many human resource organizations to play may be in TQM training.

Regardless of the institution's commitment to TQM, any organization, groups of individuals, or a solitary convert can practice TQM in their sphere of influence. The same is true for those interested in planning. While institutional commitment and practice of these management principles may be highly desirable, it is not an absolute necessity. The task of living these principles may be more difficult when needing to interface with individuals or units who or which have not embraced these concepts. However, there is always the opportunity to persuade others of the merits of these concepts through the successful pursuit of and corresponding results from these management philosophies.

Issues that organizations face in developing a supportive environment for quality include the struggle between providing what is needed without creating a bureaucracy that is the antithesis of TQM. Additionally, organizations need to be wary of creating separate organizations to "do quality" since others in an organization may view that as relieving them of responsibility for quality.

One of the early adopters of TQM is Oregon State University (OSU), which began the introduction of TQM principles and concepts via the training organization in the human resource department. At the onset of OSU's TQM initiative, the individual appointed as "quality manager" reported to the director of human resources. As TQM process improvement activities expanded beyond the support areas under the vice president for administration—who was the university's initial champion—the quality manager's sphere of involvement also broadened. Today she reports directly to the president—a testimony not only to the importance the president accords TQM but also to the current quality manager's abilities to practice and teach the principles.

In the Maricopa Community Colleges District in Phoenix, Arizona, the human resource division evolved into the Quality and Employee Development group that houses the quality initiative among its many responsibilities. They view quality as a people issue and since human resources is concerned with people, there was a natural affinity to align TQM with human resources. Believing cultural change occurs as human resources are managed and viewed by others, human resource planning, orientation, and training are key to their quality initiative.

Institutions with strong, successful, and credible human resource development functions can leverage those organizations into being a major player in fostering cultural change. That change is the key to the successful adoption of TQM principles and concepts.

Conclusion

In summary, an organization can enhance the strategic planning process through the adoption of TQM. TQM adds the element of customer satisfaction to the process to ensure organizational vitality and mission focus. TQM provides a scientific method (PDCA) to guide process improvements that the planning activities identify as critical to the success of the organization. Furthermore, TQM enhances the implementation of planning activities through the use of quality improvement teams.

Notes

1. Port, O. and J. Carey. "Quality: A Field With Roots That Go Back to the Farm." *Business Week, Bonus Issue,* 25 October 1991, p. 15.

2. Port and Carey, "Quality: A Field With Roots That Go Back to the Farm."

3. Dobyns, L. and C. Crawford-Mason. 1991. *Quality or Else: The Revolution in World Business.* Boston, MA: Houghton Mifflin Company.

4. Dobyns and Crawford-Mason, *Quality or Else.*

5. Juran, J. M. 1989. *Juran on Leadership for Quality: An Executive Handbook.* New York: Free Press, p. c-3.

6. Crosby, P. B. 1984. *Quality Without Tears.* New York: McGraw-Hill, p. 59.

7. Gitlow, H. S. and S. J. Gitlow. 1987. *The Deming Guide to Quality and Competitive Position.* Englewood Cliffs, NJ: Prentice-Hall, p. 35.

8. Enarson, H. 1983. "Quality—Indefinable But Not Unattainable." *Educational Record,* 64 (1), p. 7-9.

9. Garvin, D.A. 1988. *Managing Quality: The Strategic and Competitive Edge.* New York: The Free Press.

10. Gitlow and Gitlow, *The Deming Guide,* p. 19.

11. Collins, J. C. and J. I. Porras. 1991. "Organizational Vision and Visionary Organizations." *California Management Review,* 34 (1), p. 30-51.

12. Sherr, L. A. and G. G. Lozier. 1991. "Total Quality Management in Higher Education." In *Total Quality Management in Higher Education,* ed. L. A. Sherr and D. J. Teeter, New Directions for Institutional Research, no. 71. San Francisco: Jossey-Bass, p. 8.

13. Scholtes, P. R. et al. 1988. *The Team Handbook: How to Improve Quality with Teams.* Madison, WI: Joiner.

14. Senge, P. M. 1990. *The Fifth Discipline: The Art & Practice of The Learning Organization.* New York: Doubleday.

15. Senge, *The Fifth Descipline,* p. 13.

16. Selznick, P. 1957. *Leadership in Administration: A Sociological Interpretation.* New York: Harper & Row, p. 54.

17. McCloskey, L. A. and D. N. Collett. 1993. *TQM A Basic Text: A Primer Guide to Total Quality Management.* Methuen, MA: GOAL/QPC, p. 9.

References

Deming, W. E. 1986. *Out of the Crisis*. Cambridge, MA: Center for Advanced Engineering Studies, Massachusetts Institute of Technology.

Deming, W. E. 1982. *Quality, Productivity, and Competitive Position*. Cambridge, MA.: Center for Advanced Engineering Studies, Massachusetts Institute of Technology.

Miller, Richard I., ed., *Applying the Deming Method to Higher Education: For More Effective Human Resource Management*. 1991. Washington, DC: College and University Personnel Association.

8

Keeping the Plan Alive

K. Scott Hughes

Strategic planning is a process where the action of implementing is more important than the plan itself. Implementation requires that everyone within the organization works together to achieve positive results. The concepts of team work, networking, effective and open communication systems, and delegated authority and accountability are critical to successful implementation of the strategic plan.

The previous chapters dealt with the planning process. This chapter discusses what happens once the plan is approved and emphasizes the human resource professional's important role of supporting the leadership of the institution during implementation.

Implementing a new strategic plan is not done in a vacuum as though business has not gone on before. Each institution has a long history of culture and traditions that predetermines people's values, biases, and "the correct ways of doing things" that are difficult to change. It is naive to talk about implementing a strategic plan without recognizing the overwhelming importance of the way things have been done in the past and are done currently.

The previous chapters emphasize that strategic planning in today's environment is focused on substantive change. Academic institutions are trying to redefine themselves in such terms as quality customer service, productivity improvement, market relevancy, cost containment, diversity management, etc. Academic institutions are attempting new methods for delivery of academic services, adapting to the latest technologies, and identifying new education markets while at the same time trying to sustain the traditional academic cultural values of faculty tenure and faculty independence.

Institutional leaders who are serious about changing their organizations to adapt to the demands of the twenty-first century are using their strategic plans to forge a consensus on what the future should and will look like.

Institutional leaders who are serious about changing their organizations to adapt to the demands of the twenty-first century are using their strategic plans to forge a consensus on what the future should and will look like. The human resource professional is a key member of the leadership team responsible for the implementation and ultimate success of the plan.

Underlying Assumptions in the Strategic Plan

Implementing the strategic plan requires assumptions about what the plan is expected to accomplish. The following assumptions recognize many of the issues facing colleges and universities today and have been discussed at length in the previous chapters.

The Strategic Plan Aims to Change the Culture of the Institution. Organizational design is undergoing a shift as massive as that brought on by the assembly-line concept of the early twentieth century. Technological advancements in desktop computing coupled with the startling advancements in communications are making bureaucratic command and control structures obsolete virtually overnight.

Electronic methods of processing and communicating information are eliminating most manual operations, changing the composition and nature of the administrative work force, and redefining the way people do business. The distribution of increased knowledge and elimination of most manual processing operations increase the delegation of responsibility, authority, and accountability of personnel throughout the institution.

The Strategic Plan Requires Bold Leadership. Institutional change requires leadership willing to take chances and capable of building teams that will execute the plans. Leaders must have the vision of where they are going and possess the skills to motivate their constituencies to move in that direction.

The Strategic Plan Requires Training and Development of the Institution's Human Resources. Today's work force is ill-equipped to adapt to the redefined workplace of the next century. Skill building capabilities ranging from the technical to the interpersonal will need to be developed and integrated into the day-to-day work schedule of all members of the work force.

The Strategic Plan Expects Performance and Accountability. Implementing the strategic plan will require competent and meaningful performance assessment and evaluation to support the increased levels of accountability distributed throughout the institution.

The Strategic Plan Strives for Continuous Improvement. Maintaining the status quo is not going to be an acceptable way to operate an academic institution regardless of its current success. Assessment of current performance must be the basis for identifying new ways to improve quality, become more productive, and strive to better serve constituent interests.

Strategic Plan Implementation

Implementation of the strategic plan is discussed using the graphic outline shown in Exhibit 1. The implementation process is separated into four parts:

— translate strategies into actions;

— translate actions into results;

— translate results into assessments; and

— translate assessments into new strategies.

Translate Strategies into Actions

Strategic plans normally are expressed in terms of a specific set of strategies such as: Increase enrollments by x percent, raise academic standards to achieve y achievement scores, eliminate some academic programs while starting others, identify and secure new funding sources of z million, etc.

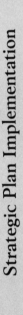

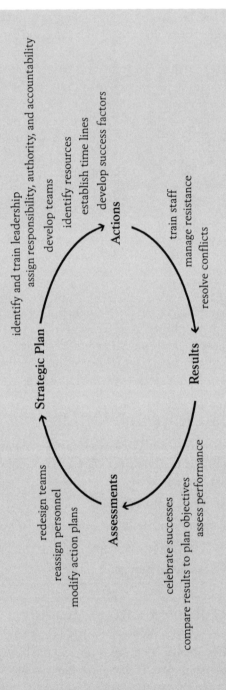

Exhibit 1

Strategic Plan Implementation

In some cases, the strategic plan has been thoughtfully crafted and extensive research, analysis, and debate already has taken place so that the faculty, staff, students, and alumni have had a chance to participate and are prepared for the implementation phase. In other cases, the development of the strategic plan may not have had such widespread participation and an extensive "selling" effort will be required.

Translating strategies into actions is the *organizational phase* of the implementation process. Key aspects of the organizational phase are: identify and train leadership; assign responsibility, authority, and accountability; develop teams and networks; identify operating resources and investments; establish time schedules and allocate resources; and develop critical success factors.

Identify and Train Leadership. Good leaders can overcome poor plans while poor leaders can defeat good plans. The beginning point of the strategic plan's implementation is a critical assessment of the leadership qualities of the organization, including the quality of the governing board. The leadership qualities of the chief executive officer, chief academic officer, chief financial officer, and chief development officer also must be evaluated.

External assessments as well as self-assessment processes should be undertaken on a frequent basis to evaluate the strengths and weaknesses of the leadership team. Where weaknesses exist, training and development resources need to be invested, job responsibilities redefined, or new leaders identified who are capable and willing to execute the strategic plan.

The leadership team also must be able to work together. Ongoing team building, skill training, and development exercises should be a routine part of the work schedule of the governing board and senior staff leadership.

The leadership of the institution has the responsibility to show commitment to the strategic plan. Beginning with the chief executive officer and the governing board, the strategic plan needs to have high visibility and priority. Several key concepts are important at this stage:

— Leadership needs to express to each succeeding level of directors, managers, supervisors and administrators a sense of commitment and responsibility for implementing the plan. The chief executive of the institution can be effective only if he or she gains the support of each managerial level in the organization.

— Communication needs to be open and frequent. Everyone in the institution should be aware of the changes that are being made and progress to date. Open lines of communication should be encouraged providing maximum amounts of accurate information.

— Institutional leadership must give continual reinforcement to the need for and benefits of change. Over time the urgency of the strategic plan will wane as the inherent difficulties of implementation take effect and as resistance builds to the effects of the changes. Frequent references to the consequences of not changing (i.e., continuing budget deficits, regulatory noncompliance, increasing customer complaints, etc.) should be made.

Assign Responsibility, Authority, and Accountability. The strategic plan takes on substance when people are given the responsibility and authority to change what they are doing currently to what is expected by the plan.

Implementation of the strategic plan may require that new job descriptions be written and new organizational structures be put in place at the beginning of the process. Realistic assessments of individual workloads should be made and release time should be given when additional workloads are deemed too onerous.

Develop Teams and Networks. The ultimate success of the strategic plan rests with the work force of the institution. Leaders need to identify teams responsible for carrying out the actions described by the strategic plan. The teams should represent the varying interests of the constituencies who will be affected by the plan.

For example, assume the strategic plan calls for new human resource systems that redesign job classification structures, performance expectations, and incentive compensation provisions to reflect changes in the way work is organized and performed. Teams involving a broad cross section of the work force need to be formed to participate in the analysis, evaluation, and eventual implementation of the new human resource systems.

Communications systems such as e-mail and bulletin boards also need to be in place so that all team members can be reached and kept up to date on key issues.

Identify Operating Resources and Investments. Implementation of the strategic plan may require additional operating resources and investments that need to be identified. Consulting assistance, investment in new technologies, and temporary help to offset release time are typical incremental costs that need to be considered.

Institutional leadership must give continual reinforcement to the need for and benefits of change.

In many cases, these onetime costs may be recoverable in cost savings and productivity improvements once the strategic plan is implemented fully. The strategic plan may regard the future cost savings as funding sources for the onetime investments required to implement the plan.

Establish Time Schedules and Allocate Resources. Rigorous monitoring and controls need to be exercised over the implementation effort. Detailed time-phased work plans identifying specific tasks and actions need to be developed. Specific individuals need to be given primary responsibility for completing each action. Intermediate milestones and firm completion dates need to be defined and agreed on by everyone involved in the implementation effort.

Resources that have been allocated to the implementation effort should be sequestered and separately budgeted and accounted for and reported on a frequent basis.

The detailed work plan and time schedule should be updated on a frequent basis, at least monthly, and used as the basis for formal status reports that are available to everyone in the institution.

Develop Critical Success Factors. It is important to know when implementation of the strategic plan has been successful. Quantitative measures of success, such as new enrollment levels, fundraising goals, reduced staffing levels, etc., should be identified early in the implementation process. Throughout the implementation process, the targeted goals give direction and reinforcement to the strategic plan. Progress can be measured easily. Periodic reassessments can be made to reevaluate whether the objectives of the strategic plan are feasible and realistic.

Role of the Human Resource Professional in Translating Strategies into Actions

1. Identify team-building and leadership development resources, such as training programs, seminars, and external consultants that can be used by the chief executive and board to evaluate current leadership quality and implement ongoing leadership training programs;

2. Evaluate the institution's current position description and job classification systems to be sure they have the flexibility to adapt to the changing work force and the new organizational design concepts of networks and team building. If new systems are necessary, begin the process of evaluating alternative human resource management systems;

3. Be a resource to the institutional leadership for developing the implementation teams. Help define the responsibilities of the teams, how they will interact, and the overall management and control systems that need to be in place for the teams to coordinate their efforts; and

4. Actively participate on the implementation teams that will involve human resource management issues.

Translate Actions into Results

The organizational stage of the implementation effort is soon taken over by rounds of meetings, data analysis, and re-organization efforts that are evidence changes are being made and that new initiatives have been started. Achieving the desired results of the strategic plan requires day-to-day activity and the culmination of many individual decisions that ultimately lead to successful accomplishments.

Important activities during the *operations phase* of the strategic plan's implementation are: train and develop staff, manage resistance, and resolve conflicts.

Train and Develop Staff. Ultimate success of the implementation effort rests on the capabilities and motivation of the people who work in the organization. Individuals need to have a clear understanding of their role in the institution and what is expected of them. They need to understand how their work efforts relate to others in the organization, who relies on them, and how they rely on others.

Training programs need to be in place that build the technical skills directly related to the individual's job and interpersonal skills such as communication, team building, supervision, leadership, etc. The training program should be tailored to the needs of each individual based on the person's current position and responsibilities, existing skill sets, and expected future performance. Individualized training and development plans should be in place with specific goals and achievement levels defined.

Training and development activities should be an integral part of the job content of all personnel. Accomplishments toward meeting the training and development goals should be monitored closely to be sure the skill set of the total work force continues to improve.

When implementation of the strategic plan requires new skills, the training and development programs should be modified for the individuals affected by the new changes.

Manage Resistance. Implementing the strategic plan is bound to create resistance from large numbers of individuals in the work force. As the plan becomes operational, decisions will be made and actions taken that change the status quo.

Be a resource to the institutional leadership for developing the implementation teams.

Many will feel their job threatened, diminution of responsibility and authority, effect on career growth and advancement, salary level, etc. Others simply will feel insecure when any change takes place, even if the change is benign.

If resistance is allowed to build, it can coalesce and become a major deterrent to accomplishing the aims of the strategic plan. Resistance from each individual needs to be anticipated and dealt with early in the implementation process and continually throughout until the changes have been fully integrated into the operations of the organization.

The key ways to deal with resistance are:

— Continually reinforce the benefits resulting from the implementation effort. They may include the improved financial condition of the organization, an increased reputation for quality, and better opportunities for career growth and personal advancement. Show that the future offers opportunities that cannot be achieved under present conditions.

— Reinforce the consequences of not making the changes. Increased budget reductions, job losses, and poor working conditions are current examples of what can occur when strategic plans fail. Individuals need to understand that the current conditions will worsen if the strategic plan is not implemented.

— Relate to the individual motivations of each staff person. Some people see change as exciting and look for opportunities for personal advancement. Others see change in a much more negative light and for many different reasons. Communication regarding the effect of the strategic plan's implementation needs to be tailored to address the fears and aspirations of each individual in the organization. Day-to-day supervisors should be thoroughly trained and kept informed of the status of the implementation effort.

Resolve Conflicts. Implementing the strategic plan may create conflict among members of the work force. Conflicts may arise between individuals as they compete to protect their status or seek to improve their position in the organization. Conflicts also may arise among groups of people, often involving bargaining groups or labor unions charged with protecting work rules and representing the interests of specific members of the work force.

Conflict resolution among employees is probably the most difficult aspect of implementing large-scale changes in an institution. Important points to keep in mind when resolving conflicts are:

— Anticipate that personnel conflicts will occur. Realize in advance that proposed changes may raise anxieties, fears, and hostility among some members of the work force. Do not be surprised and caught off-guard when proposed changes are met with either aggressive or passive resistance.

— Appoint outspoken individuals expected to be critical of change when forming the implementation teams. The potential critics will have an opportunity to see how the change process is working and become active participants in the process rather than be after-the-fact critics that could sabotage implementation.

— Keep all personnel informed of the status of the implementation effort. Use open meetings to give status reports and to invite employee comments, suggestions, and criticisms. Create a newsletter or have a regular column in an existing internal periodical that routinely describes events and accomplishments of the implementation effort.

— Thoughtfully listen and consider the criticisms being voiced. Frequently, substance can be found within the criticisms and should be incorporated into the implementation process. Openly acknowledge the importance of the suggestions and criticisms that have been made.

Finally, even after investing major effort to resolve conflicts, some issues may prove impossible to resolve. They may involve potential layoffs, reductions in pay, changes in work rules, loss of benefits, etc. These are issues that can only be resolved through institutional processes such as grievance proceedings or mediation hearings. The objective of the implementation plan is to reduce to the absolute minimum the number of conflicts or disputes that cannot be worked out in advance through the techniques described previously.

Role of the Human Resource Professional in Translating Actions into Results

1. Develop and advocate a comprehensive staff training and development program integral to each individual's job responsibilities. Implement human resource policies and programs that assess the training and development needs of each employee, set achievement goals, and monitor and evaluate performance toward expectations;

2. Assist institutional leadership in understanding how and why resistance may occur during the implementation process. Help identify the individuals that may require special efforts in understanding and adapting to the changes. Provide

guidance and offer counseling resources to individuals who may seek assistance during the implementation efforts. Participate in the efforts to show employees the benefits resulting from the change and the consequences that may result if the implementation effort fails; and

3.   Establish grievance and mediation services of the highest professional competency. Provide training and development programs to supervisors and managers to build their human resource skills so they are knowledgeable about the dispute resolution processes.

Translate Results into Assessments

The prior steps in the implementation process address the *organizational* and *operational phases*. The third step is the *assessment phase*. At this point, critical evaluations are made to decide how effective the implementation effort has been to date. The assessment process is an ongoing activity throughout the implementation stage. Assessments can take place during the course of daily work, at monthly status meetings, at the end of each term or semester, and annually. The point is not to wait until the plan is over to determine the success of the results.

Key aspects of the *assessment phase* are: assess performance, compare results to plan objectives, and celebrate successes.

Assess Performance. Assessing performance involves the measurement of actions taken compared with previously determined expectations. For example, a performance goal may have been set to increase student retention rates by implementing new student services programs and improving the quality of recreational facilities. Determining whether the new student services programs and recreational facilities have been completed on time, to specifications, and within budget is performance assessment.

Each individual who participated in the team effort to create the new student services programs and build the recreation facilities needs to be evaluated on an ongoing basis throughout the implementation process. Continual feedback is important to recognize and encourage excellent performance and to be able to take early corrective action when problems occur.

Compare Results to Plan Objectives. In the student retention rate example, performance assessment concentrated on the completion of the tasks as described in the implementation plan. The second part of the assessment process compares actual results to the original plan objectives. Even though the student services programs and recreation facilities may have been completed as planned, they still may not have the desired effect on retention rates.

The separation of assessments between tasks completed and results achieved is important. Individuals and teams may be highly successful in completing their tasks as defined but may be less than successful in accomplishing the anticipated results. Continual monitoring of performance compared with expected results throughout the implementation process is critical to minimize the ineffective use of human and financial resources.

Celebrate Successes. When people are successful, they need to celebrate. Everyone enjoys the thrill of victory—knowing he or she has done a job well and has been recognized for it. Throughout the implementation process, special note needs to be made of those accomplishments. They may seem relatively minor—receiving a letter from a grateful parent, the completion of a laboratory remodeling project, a successful fund raising event—but when these successes do occur, they need to be publicized and everyone made to feel their efforts and contributions were important to the success.

Role of the Human Resource Professional in Translating Results into Assessments

1. Ensure that performance assessment systems are in place to facilitate the ongoing assessment process throughout the implementation effort. The systems need to track, for each individual and teams, the performance expectations and status of activity;

2. Offer training and development programs to assist supervisors and managers in the performance assessment process. Include material on how to establish original goals, when to offer feedback on performance, how to offer constructive criticism when improvement needs to happen, and when

Ensure that performance assessment systems are in place to facilitate the ongoing assessment process throughout the implementation effort.

expectations may have to be modified due to unexpected results; and

3. Assist in establishing activities that recognize suc-
    cesses. They may be special award ceremonies rec-
    ognizing outstanding performance, newsletter
    articles that describe recent accomplishments, or
    simply seeing that letters are sent by the chief ex-
    ecutive to individuals who performed a special
    service.

Translate Assessments into New Strategies

The *assessment phase* of the strategic plan implementation
process determines how successful those involved have been
in meeting the original objectives. Results will be a combination of successes and failures; rarely will everything attempted
be accomplished on the first try. The final stage of the implementation process takes what we learned to modify and adapts
our approach. This step of the implementation process is called
the *adjustment phase*.

Key aspects of the *adjustment phase* are: modify action plans,
reassign personnel, redefine workloads, and redesign implementation teams.

Modify Action Plans. When it is learned during the assessment process that something is not working, the approach
needs to be changed and work continued toward meeting goals
or accepting the fact that the original objectives may not be
achievable. Deciding which course of action to take requires
sound analysis and judgment on the part of the institution's
leadership. Important steps to consider are:

— Reexamine the underlying assumptions of the strategic plan. What may have been assumed to be true when
   the plan was developed may no longer be accurate.
   For example, fund raising campaigns are built on a
   large number of working assumptions—size of prospect pool, giving patterns, general economic conditions, etc. Throughout the campaign effort, the
   assumptions need to be reexamined continually to see
   if the original campaign goals continue to be realistic.

If the original assumptions change, they may cause the original goals to be modified.

— Survey clients and constituents. If the strategic plan is intended to change client or customer behavior, continually survey the population to be sure the results are as intended. For example, if the strategic plan is intended to improve dormitory living conditions as a way to stimulate enrollments, ongoing surveying is necessary to be sure that the students' behavior patterns are indeed changing as anticipated. The survey results may indicate that the improved living conditions did not materially affect the preference choices of the students, requiring a different approach to improving enrollments.

— Increase the amount of resources allocated to the implementation effort. The original estimates for the resources required to accomplish the strategic plan objectives may have proven faulty. For example, the technical aspects of a technology systems implementation may have been underestimated, requiring additional external consulting or capital investment. New budgets may need to be created, as well as extending time schedules to reflect the expansion of the scope of the implementation effort.

The decision to stay the course and strive to meet the original objectives or admit they are not within reach requires the judgment and wisdom of the leadership and is one of the most difficult aspects of their job.

Reassign Personnel. The assessment process may reveal the original assignment of staffing needs to change. Ongoing evaluation of individual performance will show which individuals are excelling and those who are not meeting expectations. By rearranging staffing, skill sets can be matched better to the requirements of the implementation effort.

Human resource systems need to be flexible enough to allow the movement of personnel within broad work classification groupings to allow for the free exchange of positions. Rigid and narrowly defined job classification structures based on extensive job content audits and preapproval processes will not be constructive when trying to implement broad-based changes in an institution.

Participate in the assessment of the effectiveness of the teams as the implementation effort unfolds.

Redefine Workloads. The original assumptions regarding expected workloads also need to be revisited as a result of the assessment process. Some aspects of the implementation effort may require significantly more work to complete, such as interviews, data analysis, and training programs. Other functions may be able to be completed in less time than originally thought.

Frequently, implementation tasks for the strategic plan are added on top of existing workloads, causing increased workloads that are agreed on at the start of the process. When individuals become overwhelmed with unexpected workload demands, their workloads need to be adjusted and relief given due to the stress of overwork.

Redesign Implementation Teams. The teams originally set up to carry out the implementation effort may need adjusting. As the implementation effort progresses, the nature of the work shifts as well. For example, in the early stages, work may be primarily data gathering, interviewing, and understanding the basic issues of the assigned area. The work then moves to more quantitative analysis, problem solving, and intense discussions of alternatives. Finally training programs are put in place, new procedures implemented, and operations begun. The composition of the implementation team for the early stages of the process may need to be modified to reflect the requirements of the later stages of the implementation effort.

Role of the Human Resource Professional in Translating Assessments into Strategies

1. Offer guidance and assistance in the process to reassign personnel. Aid team leaders as they work toward deciding how best to match human resources to the tasks at hand;

2. Be sure the position classification structures and human resource systems are designed to encourage the movement of human resources within the institution; and

3. Participate in the assessment of the effectiveness of the teams as the implementation effort unfolds. The expertise of the human resource professional will be useful in assessing how effectively the teams are performing.

Implementation of the strategic plan is the most rewarding aspect of the total process. Improving service to students and faculty, increasing the financial viability of the institution, and enhancing the skills and knowledge of the work force are crucial objectives that need to be achieved by colleges and universities. The strategic planning process is the best way to accomplish those objectives.